Your Crystal Allies Endorsements

"*Your Crystal Allies: The 12 Best Gems and Minerals for Healing Trauma and Navigating Change* is the most concise collection I have read for those looking to create real healing and transformation in their lives. Tracee not only provides spiritual insight on these crystals, but also includes the important geological attributes to help readers truly to get know these crystal companions right down to their atoms. Her personal stories give insight on how crystal energies may manifest in one's life and make this book an all-around enjoyable read. No matter the level of experience, I highly recommend this book to anyone interested in working with crystals."

—**Alex Fernandez,** Owner of Hearthside Candles and Curios, Ralston, NE

"*Your Crystal Allies* is a brave offering steeped in deep wisdom and empowerment. Author Tracee Dunblazier invites the reader on a magical and unexpected journey into the insight of the Crystal kingdom. Sharing channeled crystal wisdom, personal stories, and historical context, this book acts as a dynamic healing agent for gentle and positive encounters with new trusted guides and Angels."

—**Austyn Wells,** Soul Gardener™ and author of *Soul Conversations: A Medium Reveals How to Cultivate Your Intuition, Heal Your Heart, and Connect with the Divine*

"A Delightfully Different Crystal Book! You will find this crystal book as captivating as I did. I could NOT put it down before finishing the book. The author's journey of self-discovery and healing with her master crystals is genuine, educational, and inspiring. In *Your Crystal Allies*, Tracee shares her personal experiences of how our crystal allies and their spirit guardians chose to help her and how they can help you. I highly recommend this book to anyone interested in crystal healing."

—**Anne-Marie McCormack,** Author of *Divination 101* and the *Sixth Sense Connection Oracle Cards*

GoTracee Publishing LLC
1601 Government St Suite B
Baton Rouge, Louisiana, 70802
www.BeASlayer.com

LCCN: 2022916255
ISBN: 978-0-9993623-6-5 print book
ISBN: 978-0-9993623-9-6 ebook

Editor: Stephen J. Miller at www.FaceBook.com/stephenjmilleredinting
Cover & interior Design: Nelly Murariu at www.PixBeeDesign.com
Photography: Tracee Dunblazier
              Kevin Break (Rose Quartz, Tracee Photo)

Disclaimer: Tracee Dunblazier is not a medical doctor and does not offer medical diagnosis or therapy. No information and opinions offered through this title, through GoTracee Publishing LLC., GT Publishing, GTP, or through any other venue representing Tracee Dunblazier are to be substituted for appropriate mental health or medical help. In no event are Tracee Dunblazier, her agents and/or representatives liable for any damages whatsoever arising out of or in any way connected with any individual's interpretation or use of information contained in this title. By reading this title you recognize and agree to take complete and total responsibility for yourself, your experience, and your actions.

Publisher's Cataloging-In-Publication Data

Names: Dunblazier, Tracee, author.

Title: Your crystal allies : the 12 best gems and minerals for healing trauma and navigating change / Tracee Dunblazier.

Description: Baton Rouge, Louisiana ; Los Angeles, California : GoTracee Publishing LLC, [2022] | Series: Your crystal allies series | Includes bibliographical references.

Identifiers: ISBN: 978-0-9993623-6-5 (print) | 978-0-9993623-9-6 (ebook) | LCCN: 2022916255

Subjects: LCSH: Quartz crystals--Therapeutic use. | Gems--Therapeutic use. | Minerals--Therapeutic use. | Energy medicine. | Psychic trauma--Alternative treatment. | Spiritual healing. | Change (Psychology) | Grief. | Divination. | Chakras. | LCGFT: Self-help publications.

Classification: LCC: RZ415 .D86 2022 | DDC: 615.852--dc23

YOUR CRYSTAL ALLIES

Anne —
10,000 Blessings
to you!
TD

The 12 Best Gems and Minerals
for Healing Trauma
and Navigating Change

Tracee Dunblazier

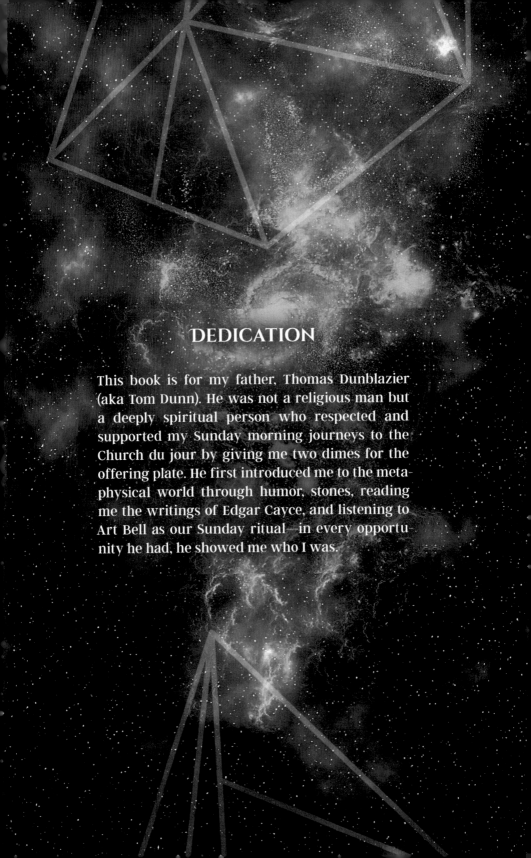

DEDICATION

This book is for my father, Thomas Dunblazier
(aka Tom Dunn). He was not a religious man but
a deeply spiritual person who respected and
supported my Sunday morning journeys to the
Church du jour by giving me two dimes for the
offering plate. He first introduced me to the metaphysical world through humor, stones, reading
me the writings of Edgar Cayce, and listening to
Art Bell as our Sunday ritual—in every opportunity he had, he showed me who I was.

CONTENTS

FOREWORD
BY KATHERINE SKAGGS

I have had a love affair with crystals and stones since early in life. As a child, I would pick up rocks on the walking path or on the land of our farm we visited on weekends. Everything became more interesting when I found that every stone and crystal had spiritual meaning and purpose. My complete adoration of the stone beings only increased when I began to buy crystals for other people through the metaphysical store that I opened in 1993. Working with wholesale dealers allowed me to purchase multiple boxes of crystals at a time, while knowing they were enroute to someone special who couldn't wait to meet them.

As you may imagine, I indeed purchased plenty of crystals for myself too. Every crystal speaks to me through its beauty, its energy, and its consciousness. Sometimes I feel it. Sometimes its beauty and sparkle won't let me walk away. Other times I can hear its voice tell me to take it home and work with it in a particular way. Even when I hesitate to spend the money, the stone relentlessly communicates with me, so I understand that it is there for me.

For many years I relied on different books and sources of information to supplement my connection to and knowledge of the gems and minerals. However, I can't recall when anyone specifically channeled a book of crystals to address trauma and transition with the voice of the stone itself, and the personal healing experiences Tracee brings to each of us. So it is a pure delight to read Tracee Dunblazier's book *Your Crystal Allies: The 12 Best Gems and Minerals for Healing Trauma and Navigating Change.*

Tracee Dunblazier speaks directly with each stone being, through her gift of channeling. One of the things I love most about the transmission we call this book is that Tracee brings you the voice and consciousness of each Quartz variation crystal. You hear directly from its essence, who it is, its purpose, and how it is in service to assist you and all of humankind. It tells you how it is here to help us achieve our multi-dimensional ascension. The spirit of each stone is personable, loving, and illuminating. Each one clearly wants to help us move to more significant states of peace and joy.

Though this is my favorite part with each member of the rock kingdom, Tracee gives much more vital information to help expand your understanding of the stone and their journey to find you. You will discover the history of each one, including their physical properties and how they work energetically. And, of course, Tracee brings in a depth of metaphysical properties and elements that is difficult to find elsewhere. It is clear that Tracee assimilates the energy and wisdom of each crystal so she may share in an easily readable manner for both the lay person and the expert stone aficionado. Her channeled connection with the stone kingdom translates the vibration through the words and images making it easy to receive on all levels of consciousness.

Next, you will find additional in-depth healing and spiritual properties, a list of keywords associated with each stone and breakout information on how the stone can help with the body, the mind, and the spirit. You will find the ability to go deep with each stone and how it can support you physically, mentally, emotionally, and spiritually.

Tracee also gives sound advice on the care and use of each stone. She helps you embrace that you are the steward of your gems and minerals and offers specific instructions for working with each one. Learning to care for your stones is an essential part of your relationship with the physical and spiritual aspects of each. You will receive everything from how to clean your stones to offering them ritual smoke and prayer for energetically connecting. To help you work with each one, Tracee gives guidance on how to create a crystal grid for healing. This instruction assists you in becoming more masterful in shifting spaces energetically, and to clean and clear areas that bring energy in to reset the space. Tracee offers rituals to companion the stone beings, and assist you in living your most sacred life while vibrating upwards in your consciousness and body.

Another favorite part of *Your Crystal Allies* is how Tracee shares her personal story with every stone. She describes her vulnerable experiences in how the crystal helped her, taught her, brought healing, and communicated with her. Tracee's personal stories are impactful and relatable, significantly as each stone helped during unexpected family deaths and transitions. Every story tells something important about our human experience and what we must face in loss, change, grief, and trauma. No matter how spiritual we are, we need help along our journey as humans.

Through Tracee's stone journeys, she shares the insights given about the Fifth Dimension and the global shifts we are undergoing in our world today. These experiential awarenesses are an essential part of this book, for they help us understand the time we live in and what it is about from a soul's perspective. Tracee shares how crystals help us know we are in a vibrational shift and how they can help us transform. Her wisdom and insights are just what we need in these times to navigate the depth of trauma we are healing personally, ancestrally, and as a species.

Suffice it to say, I love this book and recommend it whether you are new at working with crystals, specifically need it to help you with trauma and loss, or are a crystal expert. The tone and wisdom of this book speak to my heart and soul. *Your Crystal Allies: The 12 Best Gems and Minerals for Healing Trauma and Navigating Change,* is a book of wisdom for times of significant transition. The stone Beings are speaking. They are calling to all who are listening, to all who desire to transform their energy, consciousness, hearts, and physical bodies. Tracee Dunblazier has beautifully brought forth the messages and wisdom so we can all benefit, heal, and awaken.

Katherine Skaggs,
Author and Artist of the multi-award-winning book: *Artist Shaman Healer Sage: Timeless Wisdom, Practices, Ritual, and Ceremony to Transform your Life and Awaken Your Soul*

INTRODUCTION

I have always been a bit of a rockhound: a fascination as a young child, a fanaticism as a grown woman. Long before the first Obsidian pyramid I ever purchased, I was drawn to the force and light that gems and minerals sent forth into the world, and I've taken great comfort from their presence and companionship through all my life experiences. Crystals and minerals have been some of my greatest healers and teachers. The fascinating geometric figures and patterns that make up their core and repeat through the bodies of crystals taught me about myself and the Universe in which I live.

Growing up, my sister had a rock tumbler, and small tumbled stones could often be found around the house—but my real obsession began with my marble collection. I loved the steelies but was enamored with the Chalcedony, Jasper, and oh...the Botswana Agate or Quartz crystal! I could get lost for hours in the fantastical places they would take me. My collection was comprised of everything from magical glass to beautiful stone. I would spend my childhood school recesses playing and trading marbles with my friends. Later, just after high school, I remember getting the chills on my very first visit to a New York City crystal store, as I walked beyond its threshold somewhere in the West Village. I can still see it in my mind.

The first stone that caught my eye was a two-inch Gold-Lace Black Obsidian pyramid. It drew me into its history and triggered my past-life images of the Olmecs and to other South and Central American tribes whose ancient history my soul would one day reveal to me. I had to have it, but at eighteen, the forty-dollar price was a little intimidating, the store clerk was no fool, she saw the twinkle in my eye and offered me lay-away. I was hooked.

You see, when a crystal draws you into its centrifugal force, you begin a new and life-changing relationship like no other—it is a love affair that never ends, even when you are far apart. Like any other beings, stones have intelligence and personalities of their own. Though they do not ever "feel" bad, they certainly can see clearly the wonderous life we have been given on this planet and they are empathetic when they see the folly of our wisdom and our ways. The rock kingdom has been imbued with all the information we will ever need to lead successful lives, take care of Mother Earth, and experience our true human potential—if we will only receive it. We rise to our superhuman selves and beyond when we open our hearts to witnessing and balancing the past, the wonder of the present, and the profound possibilities of the future.

Crystals, gems, and minerals are an integral part of our awakening and have been used throughout history for their powerful, magical, medicinal, and transformative properties. One of the many historical references to the use of crystals comes from the Ancient Sumerians, Egyptians, and Chinese who have included gems and minerals in anything from magical rituals to traditional medicine. The Greeks, Romans, and many indigenous tribes all had spiritual and everyday uses for stones and employed them in anything from cooking, to building, to spiritual ceremony. The mines of my beautiful Gold-Lace Obsidian can be found in Mexico.

Stones have played a part in all religions, and are mentioned throughout many religious texts. Did you know the origin of birthstones comes from the Bible? Aaron, the elder brother of Moses was a High Priest and used different gems and minerals in his breastplate for wellness and protection. In the Quran, it is said the sixth level of heaven, Daqua, where Moses can be found, is composed with Gold, Garnets, and Rubies. Many Eastern religions have reverence for a divine tree of life made of stone called Kalpataru. I could go on, but suffice it to say the power of gems and minerals have always been recognized and utilized for their usefulness, spiritual powers and beauty. They are an extension of the essence of the Cosmos and Mother Earth, and offer many ways to sustain humankind.

I have been attuned to many crystalline forms and receptive to their healing stories. I have worked with gem and mineral energy in every mode possible, from direct contact to elixirs made by the light of the Moon. My favorite forms of working are through altar building, meditation, and crystal grids, but nothing beats the transformative experience of sleeping and dreaming with these crystal beings.

In the experience of loss, grief, trauma, and transitions of any kind—crystal work is invaluable. Gems and minerals can partner you in any way you might need. There are crystals that will help to transform your grief, sooth your broken heart, find acceptance in what is and what is to come, and finally, they can offer you energetic historical information and download to your spirit a new path to peace just for you.

Grief is the process we have as humans to reveal needed change and to scrub the heart and brain of old, outmoded ways of thinking and being. It is through our tearful conveyance of sorrow that our neural circuitry can erase the old information and create space for new thought forms to take hold. This is how we process grief, change our heart and mind, and transform our lives.

In, *Your Crystal Allies: The 12 Best Gems and Minerals for Healing Trauma and Navigating Change,* I'd like to tell the ancient and modern stories of the twelve crystalline and mineral beings I have favored during times of tumult, transition, or sorrow. I will channel directly from each of my twelve specimens their own story from their words, their energetic history, how they can serve you through your grief process, and the ways they can impart wisdom and comfort through your current transformation.

Each chapter of this book contains a channeling from the crystal itself (in the "Stone Speaks" section) telling you about its nature and its properties. It also includes: a historical section; the healing and spiritual properties of the gem or mineral; key words to identify its medicine for you; its geological properties; my story with the stone; its care and use; and lastly, a crystal grid formation you can use at home for your own healing. I include specific information about the stone's geological properties: class (type of group); chemical composition (what compounds the gem or mineral is made from); color; formations (how the stone grows); luster (the way light interacts with the surface of a stone); cleavage (the tendency of certain crystals to break along definite plane surfaces—if a crystal structure has relatively weak atomic bonds, it is more likely to break along those planes); specific gravity (this refers to the weight of a stone—its relative density, or specific gravity, is the ratio of the density of a substance to the density of a given reference material, most often water); and its Mohs hardness scale (indicating the hardiness and potential use and care of a stone).

In the gem and mineral marketplace there are always a bevy of new stones that have recently been unearthed or places from the Earth's crust where new resources have made themselves known. Other mines have been closed and no new pockets have been found. Rest assured that whatever stone you need will find its way to you. Gems and minerals are never destroyed, they just move from person to person until they get where they need to go next.

Do not worry if you are unable to find a specimen to your liking of the specific crystals referenced here. You have a couple of options: At the end of each chapter, I have made recommendations of other stones that may be used instead. Also, I have captured photos of the favored stones in my collection (about which the stories in the book speak) that you may use for your altar or personal meditation. No one person owns the power of the gem or mineral for which they have been chosen for stewardship, and that stone's vibration transcends time and space, as does your true multidimensional nature. All you have to do is sit and focus your heart and mind on the picture of the stone and it will reveal its sacred medicine to you.

I'd also like to speak about other people's guidance and opinions. I have found that working in the healing industry, we all have our preferences, experiences, and beliefs. Each and every one of them will serve and advocate for the person for whom they belong, but they are never intended to become your truth. There is a lot of information in the world today about gems and minerals and their spiritual meanings; it is up to you to sift through it all and see what speaks most profoundly to your spirit.

Working with healing stones requires and teaches a new level of self-trust and intuition. Regardless of what others say, you will be attracted to, create, or harness your own relationship to the stones that speak to your soul—you can never be wrong.

Our verbal and written history is limited to the perspective of the person who brings it into the world as truth. Including mine. I can only speak to what I know to be righteous in my own heart. All gems and minerals have been in the Earth for millions of years despite our human discoveries over the past few millennia.

It is divine to listen to your own higher guidance as to what each stone can do for you and the story it will share. Please, do not let the understanding of others get in the way of your own relationship to the stones that communicate to you. Use the wisdom of others to magnify and pinpoint your own understanding of how you are to receive and work through your own traumas and transitions with your crystal allies.

Whether you are new to the world of the healing wisdom of crystals and gemstones or a veteran like myself, I hope this book will bring you some new information and inspire you to reach out to the stone kingdom with your love and your sorrow. They are always waiting to hear from you, to assist in whatever you may need.

ZAMBIAN
CITRINE

1

BARITE

2

BLUE LACE
AGATE

3

BOTSWANA
AGATE

4

SMOKY
CATHEDRAL
QUARTZ

5

DENDRITIC
QUARTZ

6

KUNZITE

7

PHANTOM
QUARTZ

8

RELATIONSHIP
QUARTZ

9

ROSE
QUARTZ

10

SELF-HEALED
QUARTZ

11

ANDARA

12

1
YOUR ALLY
ZAMBIAN
CITRINE

Connecting to the Center of the Earth

CITRINE SPEAKS

Hi, I am Citrine. Not to brag, but I am the megastar of Quartz Crystal. Everybody knows me. Understandably, I am quite versatile and am suitable for just about any situation. I have a fantastic spectrum of hues in the golden ray, anything from bright to light yellow or golden, and sometimes orange brown. I can be found all around the world at this point, and my sultry pastels or rich yellows are the most popular. I also have a strong relationship to Amethyst: we are opposites and have formed an alliance through Ametrine.

I am no stranger to big emotions. I love them, and you can give all yours to me. I help with anxiety, depression, grief, and mourning— any kind of transition. Did you get a new job, or are you dating someone new? I'm there. I help you calm the waters, remember your power, and use analysis to glean important information from the situation rather than obsess on it.

Not a lot of crystals can do what I do. I self-generate and transmute energy, so you do not need to cleanse me like other Quartz, but (I am not going to lie) I love a good salt bath or some blessing smoke from palo santo or cedar—my two favorites.

You see, the first lesson to feeling good about yourself is having respect and gratitude for others. Self-confidence is something that is cultivated, and if you are born with it, it was developed in another life experience.

It works the same way for low self-esteem, it is a habit that is practiced until it becomes a way of life. It is not how you feel about yourself; it represents the limitations in your understanding of yourself and your world, that is all. Trust me, I get what it's like to be misunderstood. Sometimes folks label me as a manifestation stone, and while that is a valuable aspect to what I do, underneath it all, I help you feel good about yourself and comfortable to be confident. I show you how to reckon having money or resources instead of just wanting them.

My motto is: "You can have it all when you can handle it all."

You are not being arrogant when you believe in yourself. And because you believe in yourself, it doesn't mean you are better than anyone else. I am not quite sure why humans confuse these things. In the stone kingdom, we don't conflate them in the same way. We recognize each crystal's specialties. Versatility is my specialty, while Rose Quartz is the megastar of love. She is, by far, the most renown crystal; everyone knows her. We love that about her. But let's take Trigonic Quartz, not too many people have heard of them. They are a specialty stone that works in very specific ways for fewer people, and there aren't as many of them around. Their niche brand (high-vibrational stones that help with resetting soul patterns) is spectacular, there is no comparison.

It is the same for humans. The self-criticism gene, or pattern in the DNA, was never meant to diminish people; it is meant to conjure and cultivate self-awareness so that humans stay in their bodies as long as possible. It is in my nature to find peace in letting people do as they will, but that doesn't mean I do not have an opinion. All the colonizing, warring, and using the illusion of God to control others is ridiculous. Yes, I can say that because I will still be here when the warring factions are gone or have destroyed everything. No matter what, I am always here.

Conflict generated outside is only evidence of discord experienced on the inside. I help balance and regulate the solar plexus chakra (third chakra) that governs the gut, kidneys, intestines, stomach, colon, liver, pancreas, and islets of Langerhans (where your fight or flight instinct is generated). Your digestion is how you process food, and the third chakra is how you process your emotion and personal power. Lean on me to show you how to develop your integrity and personal image in the world—how you put yourself out there is often how you receive things back.

It is vital you comprehend your value and make choices that respect yourself and others. When you do so, you build a spiritual and emotional strength that exudes a manifestation force that becomes the building blocks of all your relationships and your life. It is powerful stuff. When you can recognize your own soul's purpose you can envision the merit of others and their presence in your life, even in subtle ways.

I also excel in teaching the concept of mirroring (this is when you attract people, places, and things that give you clues as to your inner nature, your environment, your situation, your behavior, or your condition). It is related to synchronicity—the spiritual messages for you evidenced by simultaneous physical, mental, or emotional occurrences. When you train your intuitive awareness to pick up on subtle happenings anywhere in your space, you have an advantage. You can seize opportunities and create great things because you were the right person in the right place at the right time—not because you are better, just perfectly timed.

I love people. My love is an active love; my love is a verb. Trust me to have your back and always support you—to be truthful without judgement. Like I said, no matter what you do, I will always be here, so you might as well lean on the professionals for longevity advice.

Hey, it has been great to speak to you in this way! I look forward to meeting you, or if you are a steward of one of my many family members, it might be time for another journey together.

HISTORY

Historically, Citrine Quartz is known to have been used on the handles of swords and other ornaments for protection, from as early as 300-150 B.C.E. It quickly became known as the "merchants stone" and associated with wealth and prosperity. It has been mined on almost every continent, namely in Argentina, Bolivia, Mexico, Spain, Uruguay, Brazil, Russia, Tibet, and many countries in Africa such as Zambia and Madagascar. In certain climates it can be found growing with Amethyst, and when it is, it is called Ametrine.

Citrine Quartz colors range from yellow to light yellow, deep gold to golden or orange brown. Today, the quality of a stone's color can impact the price, as the natural deeper golden to bright yellow stones are rarer to find and have not been mined in recent decades. Citrines can come in many Quartz configurations like Self-Healed Quartz, Cathedral Quartz, Quartz Points, cut stones, and clusters. The light lemony stones are abundant and inexpensive. Golden orange-brown hues are somewhat rare colors in Citrine Quartz and referred to as Madeira Citrine, mostly found in Brazil and Zambia.

Citrine and Topaz both serve as birthstones for the month of November. Currently, most of the mined natural Citrine is light yellow in color, but with a relatively low temperature change, treated stones can produce golden yellows, and most of the brighter golden Citrine found in the gemstone marketplace is produced by treating Amethyst Quartz with heat to create Citrine.

What about treated or synthetic Citrine?

As for heat-treated Citrine: some of the dark golden-brown Citrine Geodes you find in stores today are heat-treated Amethyst that comes from eastern Brazil. There is also synthetic Citrine, which is a man-made material that has the same chemical composition, mineral structure, and optical properties as natural citrine. It is so identical, that sometimes the only way to tell the synthetic from the natural is it is too perfect, with no inclusions.

Some of these gems are grown in labs by using the hydrothermal method and are faceted with a cut that produces a brilliant color and clarity. They are mostly made in Russia. The brilliant clarity is one of the most reliable ways to separate natural Citrine from synthetic Citrine. Nanosital is a man-made synthetic and optically transparent polycrystalline material that is formed by the crystallization of glass and can be produced in multiple colors. It mimics many gems in jewelry, such as Citrine.

Ametrine (when Citrine Quartz is found growing with Amethyst) is a beautiful, rare gem, with most of the world marketed Ametrine being provided by the Anahi Mine in Southeastern Bolivia. The mine produces a variety of Ametrine Quartz, Amethyst Quartz, Citrine Quartz, and Rock Crystal Quartz. Much of the Ametrine is cut into faceted stones with equal parts Amethyst and Citrine.

Don't be concerned about the stones spiritual properties when working with a heat treated or synthetic stone, always go with your gut when it comes to choosing the best vibration for your healing journey.

HEALING & SPIRITUAL PROPERTIES

Power Joy Resources Focus Prosperity Self-Confidence Vibrant Health

Citrine has many wonderful healing and spiritual properties and is a total prosperity stone. It not only develops your attraction to the things you need in life, but it also helps to cultivate the discipline necessary to have them. It has a powerful ability to dissipate and transmute dense energy, and to inspire and activate a faster frequency from which to function. It is excellent at helping to process big emotions like anguish, grief, and depression, and in calming deep-seated rage, anger, or delusional thinking. It is an excellent stone for folks with obsessive-compulsive personality disorder (OCPD) or bipolar disorder.

Citrine also stimulates mental focus and magnifies stamina and endurance. Citrine Quartz will help any malady of the gut, improving digestion, nutrient assimilation, and elimination processes. These stones have been used to detox the mind, body, and spirit of unneeded elements, while improving the circulation of blood and flow of lifeforce energy. Citrine also strengthens and supports the immune system.

Mentally and emotionally, Citrine supports and develops your mindfulness and self-awareness. It can help with attachment or detachment—whichever structure is needed to create emotional balance. It is also a powerful teacher of self-reliance. Citrine Quartz is one of the few stones that transmutes its own energy and doesn't need to be cleansed.

This stone is aligned with the sacral and solar plexus chakras and stimulates confidence and creative expression, while enhancing your discipline and willpower.

Citrine is a master stone of finding joy in everyday tasks and allowing acceptance for every avenue on which you find yourself, even the most devastating of paths will bear some form of satisfaction, pleasure, and happiness. Citrine Quartz reveals to us how we can engender a brilliant attitude despite debilitating loss. It is a natural human trait to feel guilt for for expressing joy in times of tumult; however, guilt is only our heart crying out to relieve itself of grief and to restore itself with joy. This process makes Citrine a wonderful heart stone as well.

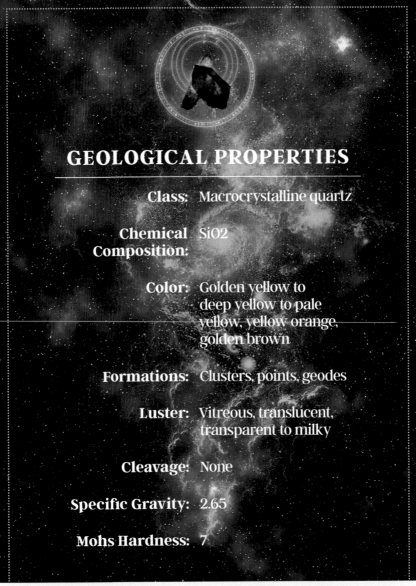

GEOLOGICAL PROPERTIES

Class:	Macrocrystalline quartz
Chemical Composition:	SiO2
Color:	Golden yellow to deep yellow to pale yellow, yellow orange, golden brown
Formations:	Clusters, points, geodes
Luster:	Vitreous, translucent, transparent to milky
Cleavage:	None
Specific Gravity:	2.65
Mohs Hardness:	7

STONES YOU CAN USE INSTEAD: Sunstone, Opal, Shungite, Leopard Skin Jasper, Tigers Eye

CARE AND USE

Citrine Quartz is a unique stone regarding its transmutation prop-erties—it doesn't need to be cleansed in the usual way. However, I do recommend you honor it for its service by bathing it in the light of the full Moon, or passing it through smoke from your sage, sweetgrass, or cedar (or whatever you or it prefers).

Citrine is a hardy stone, with a hardness level of 7, so if you drop it, it won't shatter, though it may chip or break apart. No worries: if you should drop a piece of Quartz, I always consider it synchronic-ity: taking unwanted energy and processing it through. When this happens, and the piece breaks, I take one portion and give it back to the Earth by burying it in the garden, and the other piece I keep or gift to another person.

There are many ways to use Citrine. For me, this stone is one of activity and I often carry a piece in my pocket or purse. It is wonder-ful for meditation, or to use in situations where you need to calm your nerves. It is an excellent stone when you are crying frequently or struggling to participate in life.

Placing your Citrine Quartz on your altar with a candle and prayer will amplify the intentions you set for the ritual. Sleeping with your stone will enhance your memory of dreams, and additionally, it will support your lucid dreaming or astral travel, allowing you to better visualize being the authority in your life, and setting boundaries with others who do not respect you in that way. Many folks use it as a stone of emotional protection and manifestation by keeping a piece in their water bottle for the elixir effect.

Whatever way you use Citrine, it is a powerful companion to other stones as well. Place it with Black Tourmaline for grounding and focus, or Lapis Lazuli for more direct communication.

MY ZAMBIAN CITRINE STORY

As long as I can remember, I have worked with Citrine Quartz. One of the most enduring relationships I have been in is with a Citrine. Well, there are two of them. The first I found in my original crystal shop visit in NYC. The second I discovered in a Lower East Side shop, where I met my longtime friend Russell. He owned a little metaphysical store called *Esoterica*. I loved that place.

At the time, I was new to the city, and just months before I arrived, the government had reduced mental-health funding and the local hospital Bellevue, and others, had released thousands of mental-health patients who could no longer receive subsidized treatment or housing. It was the beginning of the largest homeless epidemic ever seen anywhere, until now. Folks who needed housing but could not afford it—let alone medication—were everywhere on the streets.

I, myself, was suffering from a profound culture shock, along with chronic anxiety from a past trauma I'd experienced. To help with my endless, chaotic energy, I worked three waitressing jobs and carried a piece of Citrine with me all the time. Sometimes I would work three shifts in a 24-hour period, and it was too much to travel uptown for an hour or two, while having to be back downtown by the dinner shift, so I would walk over to *Esoterica* and chat with Russell. He was a tall, big-bellied man with long salt and peppered brown wavy hair, and he always wore several big, thick bracelets of bone and stone on both arms as well as several necklaces with two-or-three-inch gem pendants and large coral beads. I think he wore a ring on practically every finger. Often, he'd wear kaftans, but if he wore anything else, it would be cotton. He seemed like the most peaceful person in the world, until he opened his mouth. He was an activist at heart and was clearly from New Jersey.

His strong accent, with his sarcastic wisdom and occasional vulgar choice of words, had me in stitches most of the time. He would let me spend hours in his store reading, writing, crystal gazing, and occasionally napping on these 3-foot by 8-foot shelves he had in the office in the back of the store. The top shelf was usually empty, and I would crawl up there for an hour or two before he woke me up to get to work on time.

Outside, I was struggling with facing person after person, homeless through no fault of their own, and additionally, I was working through my own rage and pain of the unfairness of it all. I was often in a state of emotional upheaval, and I found that the folks on the street were the only ones brave enough to break through my traumatized persona to ask, "Hey, how are you?" Then, they would actually stop for an answer.

One day, I was headed downtown to work—doing my best to slow my breathing from the crying jag I'd been in for an hour. I got on the train, my eyes blurry from the tears and ensuing puffiness. Walking down the train car was a homeless guy I'd seen many times. He was fairly tall and moderately built with beautiful golden-brown skin and beaded dreadlocks down to the middle of his back. Often, he talked to himself and sometimes sang songs, and when the train wasn't busy, folks would avoid him like the plague. I always took a subtle comfort from his presence.

This time he sat exactly opposite me and began to speak directly to me, what I know now as channeling. To this day, I do not remember exactly what he said, but he was speaking to my soul—telling me of the Cosmos and the many beings here to protect and comfort me. He spoke of a future where my pain didn't exist, if I could just hold on a little longer. And just as he finished, the conductor called for the West Fourth Street stop; I smiled at him, my tears all dried up, and said thank you. I left the train and headed to work with a new sense of peace, calm, and hopefulness.

I don't think I saw him again after that, but I've never forgotten him or his message. He, to me, is the epitome of the essence of Zambian Citrine: a rich golden glow of inspiration and light, just right to take in and soothe your lamenting soul. It wasn't until more recently, when I saw a friend post a picture of a Zambian Citrine piece on social media, it reminded me of him. The next day, I called the store and had a piece shipped to me immediately.

I gave it a place of prominence here because the spirit of what it channels is perfect for our world which is in profound flux. The one way we are empowered is to transform ourselves, transmuting shadow into light, disease into wellness, and pain into hope. That is one thing about Citrine Quartz: It never gives up. No matter what happens, it will always be here.

NOTES

CRYSTAL GRID FOR CLAIMING YOUR POWER

Working with a crystal grid is a simple way to begin connecting with the gem and mineral kingdom. You will need the following list of items for this specific grid. You can create a crystal grid by copying the one shown on the opposite page, on any material you would like: wood, metal, copper, paper, or cloth. Scan the QR Code on page 170 for the free grid download or go here: https://traceedunblazier. com/product/your-crystal-allies-the-12-best-gems-and-minerals-for-healing-trauma-and-navigating-change/.

Next, you will create a sacred altar space by cleaning and clearing an area in your homes main room or your bedroom, on which to place the grid. Write the intention for which you will build your grid and place it on the cleared altar space, under the grid. In addition to your grid, you can include a candle, a glass of water, and a form of offering like tobacco, corn, or cornmeal.

This can be an active or passive ritual which means you can sit with your grid for a portion of time daily, weekly, or monthly (with consistency), or you may set up your grid and go about your life in a regular way. The grid works with your subconscious and aligns you to the intention you have set forth. You will receive information in your meditation or mindfully on a daily basis.

Now collect the stones listed below and place them on your grid

- **Citrine** (ten pieces) for claiming your mental, emotional, or spiritual power in the physical world. Place the ten pieces of Citrine in a circle.
- **Black Kyanite** (five pieces) for manifestation of your vision and intent. Place a stone every two stones in length, inside the circle
- **Blue Quartz** (three pieces) for comfortably expressing your creativity in a confident way. Place the three pieces in a triangular shape inside the innermost circle.

2
YOUR ALLY BARITE

Facing Your Power

BARITE SPEAKS

People may say I am "too much," "a little aggressive," or "heavy handed," but make no mistake about it—when they need me, they are glad they found me. I am good in a crisis. At the core, I am a survivalist: willing to accept things and others as they are. I specialize in confidence. Where I come from, it is not necessary to minimize yourself for any reason; in fact, it is vital that I be exactly who I am. It is the point, being who I am—I mean, not trying to be what makes others feel comfortable. I have to be just me, in exactly the condition I am in right now. You see, no matter the form I take, my energy and power are the same.

Embracing being ancient might seem a bit of a stretch to you, but the truth is our presence is never ending. And, just like you, I am ever changing and impact everything around me. In essence, I am a provoker of the truth. Whatever words you have left unspoken, I'll draw straight out of your mouth. I'll loosen them up in your heart, shake up your vocal cords, and push them right past your lips. No matter how uncomfortable it might feel, I promise you'll be better for it.

My motto is, "You can't change what you don't acknowledge."

I am especially good at helping in dire physical health situations, sometimes for healing and other times for connecting with your ancestors and preparing to begin your walk on the road of spirit. As far as I am concerned, both are sacred rites of passage, and we will certainly walk them in our own time.

I think what makes me the perfect ally in profound times is that I will be your bridge between the truth and your deepest fears and sorrows. I will help you release your emotion and find your words in a beautiful way. Most of all, I'll help you rebuild after a loss and reclaim those dreams you may feel have passed you by. No matter what seems to be happening now, your path is being cleared to achieve your soul's deepest desire, and I won't let you give up. You can lean on me until you feel safe to move in the world on your own again.

HISTORY

Barite is connected to a mineral group that includes Anglesite, Celestite, and Hashemite. Its name, Baryte, was created by Dietrich Ludwig Gustav Karsten in 1800, and over time adjusted to an American spelling "Barite." Barite takes a wide variety of forms, occurring as blade, prismatic, or often large tabular crystals. It also occurs in lamellar and fibrous crystal formations. Barite can be colorless, yellow, red, blue, green, brown, or black—depending on the included mineral content. At times, bladed or tabular crystals of Barite form a concentric pattern of increasingly larger crystals outward. This has the appearance of a flower. Some varieties of Barite can even be fluorescent.

Barite crystals have a brilliant, glassy luster and contrast nicely with the matrix of white, crystalline quartz. It's composed of barium sulfate ($BaSO_4$) and receives its name from the Greek word "barys" which means "heavy." This name is in response to barite's high specific gravity of 4.5, which is exceptional

and influenced the young man, but I found myself saying to the young man himself, "I know you are burdened with desires you believe are yours. But they are not. You must take your spirit back and cast out this demon that only seeks to create chaos in your life."

I decided to take a walk, meandering up and down the many streets of my neighborhood, trying to make sense of the dream that was still so troubling. I knew it wasn't a prophetic dream, as I'd had so many before, but I was missing some very important pieces of the story that longed to be told. Several hours later, after a call to a good friend, it became revealed.

My friend said to me, "You were sent to intervene on the situation and keep the attack from happening."

Oh my God, yes. That is what happened. In the astral realm, I became an intercedent between the victim and the man who planned to rape her. I was thrown into her body, which had been abruptly vacated by her spirit in fear, and I realized that she was just a young child! It was the reason I didn't have immediate control over the body: It wasn't mine. And it was young and undeveloped; the girl must have been under ten years of age. Similarly, a demonic spirit influenced the pedophile in the making. This piece of the puzzle made everything make sense. It was clear that I was first speaking to the entity, and then to the boy. Late that afternoon, knowing all this, I sat in communion with my piece of Barite, and called in St. Micheal and his destroyer angels on behalf of the young man, to deliver him from the entity that plagued him.

I found myself saying to him, "You now have a second chance. But you need to know, I see you, and you are seen. For every goodness you do, you will be seen, and it will be acknowledged by your world. And for every bad thing you do, you will be seen, and there will be consequences. Today you have your choice back, but it is up to you to claim authority over your domain on all levels."

Now I could let it go. I was done. I thanked Barite for guiding me through such a powerful experience, I said a prayer for the little girl and her healing, burned some Frankincense and Myrrh, and offered smoke to the piece of Barite and the Creator, and went to bed.

CRYSTAL GRID FOR TRANSFORMATION

Working with a crystal grid is a simple way to begin connecting with the gem and mineral kingdom. You will need the following list of items for this specific grid. You can create a crystal grid by copying the one shown on the following page, on any material you would like: wood, metal, copper, paper, or cloth. Scan the QR Code on page 170 for the free grid download or go here: https://traceedunblazier. com/product/your-crystal-allies-the-12-best-gems-and-minerals- for-healing-trauma-and-navigating-change/.

Next, you will create a sacred altar space by cleaning and clearing an area in your homes main room or your bedroom, on which to place the grid. Write the intention for which you will build your grid and place it on the cleared altar space, under the grid. In addition to your grid, you can include a candle, a glass of water, and a form of offering like tobacco, corn, or cornmeal.

This can be an active or passive ritual which means you can sit with your grid for a portion of time daily, weekly, or monthly (with consistency), or you may set up your grid and go about your life in a regular way. The grid words work with your subconscious and aligns you to the intention you have set forth. You will receive information in your meditation or mindfully on a daily basis.

Now collect the stones listed below and place them on your grid.

- **Barite** for transformation at the center.
- **Rose Quartz** for gentle compassion in the north.
- **Quartz** point for knowledge and connection to the Ancestors in the east.
- **Obsidian** for safety and emotional and spiritual protection in the south.
- **Carnelian** for heart purification in the west.
- **Optional:** several small citrines connecting the center Barite with all four directions.

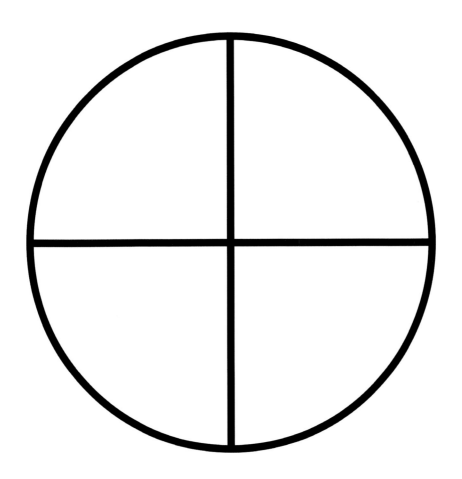

3
YOUR ALLY BLUE LACE AGATE

Combining Communication and Clarity

BLUE LACE AGATE SPEAKS

Many people do not know this, but Harmony is my middle name. It is written in my flowing blue circles and lines: there is no end, and all will be well. I come from Namibia, Africa. My sister, Blue Chalcedony, comes from Malawi, Africa. We are practically twins, but the topography where we are birthed have slight differences in the environment and minerals, which accounts for the multiple laces of blue and white we can both share.

I am a lover of life, and I don't mind talking about it. When you are near my vibration you might feel a slight opening or activation of your throat chakra right down to your higher heart chakra, which is in between the heart and throat (governing the immune system and the thyroid gland). I can be very helpful with anything concerning autoimmune or heart-related issues. The lesson I teach is about recognizing the value of direct and honest communication.

My motto is: "Just talk about it."

People naturally become calm and relaxed in my presence, and when that happens—you guessed it—communication ensues. You see, communication steadies the waters, and we are all highly aligned with water. The Earth's surface is about 70% water, and the human body is approximately 60% water, so to value water is imperative. Water carries vibration and when you are exposed to harsh emotions, they flow through every part of your body, mind, and spirit—they can sometimes lodge in your tissues and organs. Your goal is to keep the flow moving by feeling your emotions, speaking your mind, taking right action, and honoring the present.

The most loving thing you can do for another is to be honest about who you are: what it is you want; what you have done in your past; what your current condition is; and what you need now. If you are honest with others and they move away from you, they are not for you. It's that simple. The hard part, at least for humans, is accepting it.

The human body is a profound and complex structure with many moving parts, and we can help to balance all aspects of it.

One of the ways I have learned to honor the present is to recognize how I am connected to and always in communication with my environment, and therefore, impacted by it. The Sun, rain, vegetation, minerals, and movement in the Earth's crust—all these things impact my color, depth, and pattern. They form who I am. And it is valuable to remember that although I cannot make changes to these factors in my life, you can.

Another love affair I have is with the Cosmos. Like you, it is always changing—through birth, life, and death. My beautiful blue and white hues connect you with the sky and the galaxies, and they amplify your relationship to extraterrestrials. Often, you will find growing with me my best friend, a form of Quartz called Druzy. It is a mass of itty-bitty twinkling Quartz points that grow across a space, or line a Geode. You can find it on many varieties of Agate. When you find me and Druzy hanging out, we have many added superpowers. Druzy, as any good friend would, supports me—along with my balancing and energizing properties. Additionally, we can support you while you are beginning new tasks or are starting over again in some way, helping you proceed in a careful and cautious manner. We amplify your psychic abilities to channel, see, or hear energy. Also, we help keep you grounded while you are learning.

The last thing I want to say is how much I appreciate getting to be myself. I love the environment around me, the Earth that supports me, and the Cosmos that watches over me. I cherish the simplicity and complexity of it all, and just the opportunity to be here, in the present, now. If you will let me into your life, I can help you do the same.

HISTORY

Chalcedony, a variety of Quartz is one of the most plentiful and diverse stones on the planet. Agate is one of two forms of Chalcedony, the translucent one. (Jasper is opaque.) You can tell it's Agate if the light shines through. There are thousands that can be found in almost every color, and in every country on the planet. The variations in hue and pattern are really quite profound, and they all have their own spiritual meanings and healing properties.

Agates have been historically valued since the Neolithic Era. They have been used as protection and healing stones, and in magical and religious rituals—as well as being carved into everyday utility items. Agates form as nodules or geodes in igneous rocks. When the empty space of a porous rock fills with surface groundwater and dissolving silica-rich rocks, the combination will begin to crystallize, and bands of Agate form. The colors are determined by the geological environment and minerals in the ground. It is the unique combination of these factors that creates the many individual varieties of Agate.

Blue Lace Agate is found in Namibia and Zambia, with small amounts in Brazil, China, India, and the United States. Blue Chalcedony, a kindred stone, is found in Malawi. They can be visually very similar, but not the same; however, they both carry the same spiritual and healing properties. Blue Lace Agate was originally mined at Farm 254 Ysterputz, Karasburg West, near the South African border, in 1962—but it no longer mines the beautiful stone. It is believed that the presence of this Blue Lace Agate dates back 54 million years and was found deep inside a crevasse in the earth's crust.[1]

You can also find many other mineral specimens growing alongside Blue Lace Agate, including Dogtooth and other forms of Calcite crystals. Clear Quartz, Gypsum, Dolomite, Ankerite and Siderite have been found.[2]

HEALING AND SPIRITUAL PROPERTIES

Harmony	Mediator	Clarity	Unity	Hope
Inspire	Protection	Awareness		Fortitude

Blue Lace Agate is the gentlest, yet most powerful stone on the planet. Big claim, I know, but there really is not anything else that compares. When you meditate with this stone you can get swept into its translucent lines of blue and the mysteries they hold. The circular, wavy bands reconnect you with the flow of the Earth and the Cosmos, and of course, they have a strong connection to water. This stone can be a gentle diuretic, as it helps the mind and body realign with your highest vibrational possibility.

Blue Lace Agate is the stone of the mediator and strengthens communications of all kinds, on every level. It reinforces focus so you may access the right words to express your thoughts and feelings. It amplifies your telepathic abilities and awareness, and

1   Stonemania.com, 2022

2   NambianBlueLace.co.za, 2022

it strengthens your confidence in trusting the information you receive on the psychic channels. One of this unique Quartz's most valuable powers is that of the negotiator and mediator. Where there are opposing opinions, Blue Lace Agate smooths the waters. An excellent stone for anxiety and hypertension, it helps for all involved to expand their viewpoint at least enough to understand the other side of the matter, helping to ensure your words are not angry and your meaning is clear.

A teacher of unconditional love and nonjudgement, Blue Lace Agate inspires grounding, balance, and safety; with those three comes joy. This variety of Agate also supports one's ability to perceive freedom and the self-imposed walls that have prohibited that freedom in the past. It fosters serenity, which activates the immune system and generates whole body health. Additionally, it balances the chakras and the entire auric field to promote healing.

NOTES

GEOLOGICAL PROPERTIES

Class: Cryptocrystalline quartz, chalcedony, agate

Chemical Composition: SiO2

Color: Blue, white, light grey, and neutral tones

Formations: Geodes and masses

Luster: Vitreous

Cleavage: None

Specific Gravity: 2.58 - 2.64

Mohs Hardness: 6.5 to 7

STONES YOU CAN USE INSTEAD: Blue Chalcedony, Blue Quartz (Dumortierite), Sodalite

CARE AND USE

All crystals and stones may be used similarly, and their care may vary depending on the unique aspects of the stone. Blue Lace Agate is a hardy stone and is fit for many uses. You can place your Blue Lace Agate in a common room or altar area in your home to aid with effective communication between inhabitants. Or you can carry it in your pocket if you must speak or perform in public. Perhaps the most effective way to use Blue Lace Agate is by wearing it as a pendant, or in ring or bracelet form. I have always carried a piece on my person or in my bag, when going on an interview or having an important conversation with a family member or friend. Also, I use agates in my pet water fountain, as a calming elixir for my animals.

Agates can be cleansed with smoke from your favorite herb or resin like sage, cedar, or lavender; or amber, frankincense or myrrh. They are also great candidates for sunlight and moonlight cleansing, especially during a full Moon. You can use soaps and solvents to clean but should be cautious of any polish your stone may have. Trying to re-polish a stone is not a fun process if you do not have all the right tools.

MY BLUE LACE AGATE STORY

Blue Lace Agate has been a valuable ally for as long as I can remember. Helping me achieve varying levels of relief from: anxiety and rage, fear of reprisal from speaking my heart, and deep levels of attachment to any situation and its inevitable outcome. I've never sought to control other people; however, it has always been a battle within myself to control my rage when recognizing the failing of a friend or lover to be honest. The chink in the plan was in my younger days I attracted people who were as wounded as I. When faced with a difficult moment of truth within the relationship, it was easier for them, or me, to lie or say what we thought the other needed to hear.

In the past, it has been natural for people to unconsciously perceive my karmic agony, which might rise to the surface as rage from injustices dealt me. Or, to be unable to reconcile a flurry of tears from a well of previous pain, the depth of which was not rational for the situation at hand. Nobody wants to be honest in the face of such amplified, uncomfortable emotion. It was equally as frustrating for me to understand why relationships were playing out as they were: deeply connected love, yet no real environment of intimacy. These two things, working in conjunction, would not allow for the longevity it takes to form a real bond and authentic mutual respect. Many of my relationships were just partners playing out their past traumas in present-time. On some level, I knew it; however, I did not know how to stop the inevitable circumstances that would lead friends and lovers away from me.

Enter Blue Lace Agate. I have had many magnificent pieces over the years, and if memory serves me, I think my first was a piece of jewelry, a ring. This story, however, is not one of specific specimens, but the overarching impact of wearing, holding, and having the serenity of its blue and white waves of salvation consistently in my environment.

In my early twenties, I had a wonderful boyfriend, Seth. Like many of my male companions of that time he carried within him a profound capacity for compassion for me for which I was grateful. But no matter my gratitude, I struggled with my hormonal and emotional rages when I was frustrated, or things outside my control were not going my way. There is nothing like an angry tearful response to a lost set of house keys to quickly upend a potentially good relationship experience.

At the time, I was living in a rent-controlled apartment on a practically abandoned city block of Harlem. It was desolate, but unquiet—much like my furious heart. The apartment itself had a fairly large living room space, which I had made into a dance studio, replete with the standard "city linoleum" (cream-colored tiles with large dark-brown geometric shapes—think, the opposite of cool). It had bright three-foot fluorescent lights situated across the ceiling that, after a while, hurt your eyes, especially at night.

One late afternoon, Seth and I were heading out somewhere and I was about to blow a gasket because I couldn't find my keys. I was stomping around the apartment, screaming at the lost keys, when Seth gently offered his help.

I growled, "I need to find my fucking keys!"

And then for some reason, I suspect as a diversionary tactic, Seth offered to get me some coffee.

My response was, "I don't want any fucking coffee; I just want my keys!"

To his credit, he didn't tell me to relax (the worst possible thing you could say to an angry, flailing human). Naturally, this was the point where the situation would head south fast into a full-blown argument, but Seth had the patience of a Buddha, and his response caught me off guard.

"Coffee? Did I say coffee? Nobody wants any coffee here; we don't want any coffee," he said with a bright-eyed smile.

His light and humorous response stopped me in my tracks. We both burst out laughing, and for the first time I could see the ridiculousness of my displaced fury. I laughed until I cried a little, I apologized, found my keys, and we headed out for that proposed coffee.

One of the greatest lessons Blue Lace Agate has taught me over the years is the patience it takes to break down the intricate pieces of your brain's chemistry and its behavior, and their origins in your soul or present-life history.

This Agate offers the objectivity needed to see yourself and the subliminal influences that guide your thoughts and choices. One by one, it extracts them and shows them to you in the light of day. This allows you to witness their current validity, supporting you in grieving the past and helping you to choose the words and behaviors that are authentic to the present moment. It is only this process that will help your habits and brain-chemistry change from the wildly rageful manias that may plague you, to a certain and steadfast communication, as well as an emotional expression that suits the circumstances at hand.

CRYSTAL GRID FOR COMMUNICATION

Working with a crystal grid is a simple way to begin connecting with the gem and mineral kingdom. You will need the following list of items for this specific grid. You can create a crystal grid by copying the one shown on the following page, on any material you would like: wood, metal, copper, paper, or cloth. Scan the QR Code on page 170 for the free grid download or go here: https://traceedunblazier.com/product/your-crystal-allies-the-12-best-gems-and-minerals-for-healing-trauma-and-navigating-change/.

Next, you will create a sacred altar space by cleaning and clearing an area in your homes main room or your bedroom, on which to place the grid. Write the intention for which you will build your grid and place it on the cleared altar space, under the grid. In addition to your grid, you can include a candle, a glass of water, and a form of offering like tobacco, corn, or cornmeal.

This can be an active or passive ritual which means you can sit with your grid for a portion of time daily, weekly, or monthly (with consistency), or you may set up you grid and go about your life in a regular way. The grid works with your subconscious and aligns you to the intention you have set forth. You will receive information in your meditation or mindfully on a daily basis.

Now collect the stones listed below and place them on your grid.

- **Blue Lace Agate** for communication and gentleness, placed the in Center.
- **Fluorite** for a shift in thinking outside your norm, placed in the North.
- **Quartz** point for knowledge and connection to the ancestors, placed in the East.
- **Obsidian** for safety and emotional and spiritual protection, placed in the South.
- **Carnelian** for heart purification, placed in the West.

4
YOUR ALLY BOTSWANA AGATE

Courage from the Toes Up

BOTSWANA AGATE SPEAKS

People say I'm as cool and refreshing as a summer rain.

You know when you've had all the heat you can take and gently, as if awaking from a pleasant dream, a cloud moves overhead sprinkling you with fresh chilled water—just enough to invigorate your skin? Well, that is me. I was born to remove the "fight" out of anything.

Where I am from, Bobonong (in the central district of Botswana), the people are a hunting-gathering community, and the culture is an easy-going gifting society. Yes, that's right, gifting. My energy supports the idea there is more than enough for everyone. You can feel free to give to one another knowing that you will get back what you need. It will be reciprocated by your recipient or from the Universe (bringing the right people, places, and things into your life), making sure all your requirements are met.

My glorious, wavy, brown, pink, gray, and white multi-shaded stripes flow through the Earth's crust, spreading comforting vibrations everywhere I exist. Although I was born of liquid fire, I have a strong connection to water and was originally formed by the presence of the oceans' fluid swells. I remind you that your body is seventy-percent water, and I can help you keep it in balance. I also beckon to your heart and time chakras (energy centers in the body that govern compassion and spiritual history) to reveal and release their stories, whether they hold joy or pain. I can help you reconcile them on all levels with the courage of truth, the relaxation of peace, and all with the curiosity of a sexually active twenty-year-old.

My motto is, "It's all going to be all right. You can do this."

In my view, we are made of love and the giving and receiving of it is our mission. When you hold me in your hands, you will organically take the deepest breath you've taken in a while (pause for breath), and for that moment you will feel safe, warm, and nourished. Let me teach you the power of gentleness and the comfort of fluid emotional release. Let me partner you in this time of transition and help you rediscover your joy and innocence again.

HISTORY

Culled in Botswana mines, these beautiful, banded stones get their name from this landlocked democratic state near South Africa. As the name suggests, this specific material is only mined here and reflects that regarding price and availability on the world market. The most elegant of Agates, Botswana Agate is known for its history, gentleness, and beauty.

This stone is a variation of banded Chalcedony, one of the Quartz family minerals. It is often striped in different shades of cream, pink, grey, browns, oranges, and reds.

Banded Agates, in general, have been used for thousands of years (for carving cameos and other jewelry, statuary, talismans for reproductive fertility, and protection) by many cultures, not limited to its African origin but including the ancient Greeks and many others. A small ornamental carving called the "Pylos Combat Agate" is a lovely 1.5-inch gold, white, and red banded piece excavated from the Griffin Warriors tomb, dating back to 1450 BCE.

Botswana Agate is used to improve your focus and attention to detail, expand positive thoughts, and even repel a spider or two. This stone has been around for over two hundred million years and has been used for far longer than we have a history—things like protective amulets, dishes, and ceremonial and religious artifacts. Interestingly, every time I work with this stone my mouth tends to water, which pertains to one of its super-powers: it helps quench thirst.

The volcanic activity responsible for this Agate is a lava flow that moved across the landscape, settling into waves of long faults now found within layers of rock (I suspect where there was once water to cool it down). These Quartz and Silica sheets were modified over the millennia and formed the magnificent banding patterns and colors of Botswana Agate.

HEALING & SPIRITUAL PROPERTIES

Botswana Agate is beneficial for folks with a connection to fire. If you are a Leo, Aries, or Sagittarius, this is a great stone for you.

When found with its matrix (outer crust or base of the stone), Botswana Agate has a pitted, slightly translucent texture and looks somewhat like the human brain. In fact, it is thought to be supportive for brain-related conditions as it activates the crown chakra.

These stones are coveted for their ability to ground and shift any overwhelming or discordant energy. Botswana Agate is a powerful stone to use in healing spiritual maladies and influences from entities from other dimensions. It helps you claim your own physical, mental, emotional, and spiritual autonomy—shoring up your courage to gracefully set boundaries on any level necessary.

This special Agate is a natural protector and stone of solace. It can receive and transmute all the pain you have and can help you see the light at the end of the tunnel. It aids in the process and management of grief by encouraging you to feel your feelings while helping you access the time and space where the situation has changed and you are feeling inspired once again.

The patterned formation of the "eye" in a Botswana Agate can be used as the all-seeing-protective eye and a talisman for luck(!), helping you to see more and expand your awareness. This unique stone promotes composure, inner stability, and maturity. It supports the energy of safety and security and can help with deep breathing and complete exhalation.

A love drawing stone, Botswana Agate helps you to accept yourself and others exactly as you are, encouraging the freedom from expectation and judgement that often gets in the way of true intimacy with another person. By promoting alignment with your true needs, Botswana Agate helps you connect with the mate with whom you can share your true self.

NOTES

....

....

....

....

....

....

GEOLOGICAL PROPERTIES

Class: Cryptocrystalline, chalcedony, agate

Chemical Composition: SiO2

Color: Grey, brown, red, orange, with white, pink, and blue bands

Formations: Hexagonal, Geodes, masses

Luster: Waxy, greasy, vitreous

Cleavage: None

Specific Gravity: 2.60-2.65

Mohs Hardness: 6.5-7

STONES YOU CAN USE INSTEAD:
Carnelian, Ocean Jasper, Orca Agate

CARE AND USE

While agate is a resilient stone, you want to take care with this one, despite its hardness. It is not invulnerable to scratches and scuffs. If it is covered in mud and such, it is best cleaned with pure Castille soap mixed with water; otherwise, use smoke such as sweetgrass, sage, cedar, palo santo, or dragons blood and the light of the full Moon for a day or two. Do not use steam, as the stone is sensitive to heat. (Don't store in direct sunlight or the colors may fade.)

Some chemicals found in cosmetics can affect the surface polish of Agates. So, you'll want to be conscientious of spraying things like perfume, hairspray, or other hair products while wearing your favorite Botswana Agate. Store Agate jewelry in a separate pouch or box to prevent it from being scratched by other things.

Botswana Agate can be used in any way you can come up with; it is ideal as a palm stone. Use it when laying stones on your body, it can ameliorate frustration, anguish, or body pain from direct contact. Applying it with other Quartz will amplify its healing properties. Finally, wearing, holding, or producing oils and elixirs with this stone is helpful in creating balance at physical, mental, emotional, and spiritual levels.

MY BOTSWANA AGATE STORY

The year before I began working as a profes-sional spiritualist and medium was filled with many changes. I had always been psychic, but this was the first time I had been exposed to an entire community of others who similarly expe-rienced life. I was living in Venice, California, with a high school friend who was fresh out of a long-term relationship and knee-deep into a newly found sexual revolution and a romance with alcohol. I abruptly moved, sans roommate, into my own bungalow with just enough room for me and my crystals.

Just previously, I had left the restaurant industry for the final time, and soon after, another longtime job went by the wayside. I was left alone in my new little apartment with one less friend and no job. I was emotionally battered and physically exhausted, but spiritually hopeful and ready for all the new things that would soon be pouring into the void left from so many losses (the perfect scenario for Botswana Agate).

During that time, my only lifetime secret—being psychic— had been exposed. I was chatting with a co-worker about spiritual readings and let it slip that I was empathic and a medium. At this point in my life, only a few close friends knew. My co-worker immediately asked if she could pay me for a session, and next thing I knew, she began telling folks. That was the beginning of a thirty-year career of spiritual and grief counseling, and shamanic work.

I had always been a dedicated consumer at all the metaphysical shops in my community and decided to pitch several of them for a job doing psychic readings. I was successful at landing two of them. For exactly one year, seven days a week, sometimes twelve hours a day, I worked as a spiritualist, in and out of store settings. It was a time of intense self-training and self-excavation, along with learning the trade and being of service to others.

When you are immersed for so many hours of the day in a demographic of people in pain and confusion, you are challenged beyond belief with mastering your own opinions, feelings, and judgements of others—not to mention, carrying the extra-emotional weight. It requires a whole other level of self-care. This is where Botswana Agate comes in.

The store carried quite a bit of the tumbled stone, and I would bring piles of it back to my reading room. It immediately put others at ease. But mostly, it made me feel brave, confident, and comfortable—despite the constant barrage of intense emotion I communed with daily. The Agate drained the feelings of being overwhelmed right out of me, so I could be grounded for others.

At the time, there was a gentleman who worked at the store, Scott, who was a Druid (a Celtic priest) and Rune carver. He created for me a beautiful set of Botswana Agate Runes (Norse form of divination using the Norse alphabet) for which I got to choose the twenty-four pieces of stone to be carved; I then used them in client sessions. Those stones, mixed with the magick of the Norse and the wisdom of their creator, have offered me a lifetime of insight and percipience. To this day I rely on the comforting fortitude of Botswana Agate and use it in meditation when I am seeking a muse with inspiration for the future.

CRYSTAL GRID FOR COURAGE

Working with a crystal grid is a simple way to begin connecting with the gem and mineral kingdom. You will need the following list of items for this specific grid. You can create a crystal grid by copying the one shown on page 51, on any material you would like: wood, metal, copper, paper, or cloth. Scan the QR Code on page 170 for the free grid download or go here: https://traceedunblazier. com/product/your-crystal-allies-the-12-best-gems-and-minerals-for-healing-trauma-and-navigating-change/.

Next, you will create a sacred altar space by cleaning and clearing an area in your homes main room or your bedroom, on which to place the grid (found on the following page). Write the intention for which you will build your grid and place it on the cleared altar space, under the grid. In addition to your grid, you can include a candle, a glass of water, and a form of offering like tobacco, corn, or cornmeal.

This can be an active or passive ritual which means you can sit with your grid for a portion of time daily, weekly, or monthly (with consistency), or you may set up you grid and go about your life in a regular way. The grid works with your subconscious and aligns you to the intention you have set forth. You will receive information in your meditation or mindfully on a daily basis.

Now collect the stones listed below and place them on your grid.

- **Botswana Agate** (four pieces) for courage summoning, placed in the North, South, East, and West directions.
- **Prasiolite** for stability and harmony, placed in the center of the grid.
- **Carnelian** (four pieces) for physical and emotional purification of the heart. Place in the NE, NW, SE, SW quadrants of the grid.
- **Pink Calcite** (eight pieces) for cultivating compassion for oneself and others. Place in all the fixed four directions (N, S, E, W), and the cardinal directions (NW, NW, SE, SW)

NOTES

NOTES

5
YOUR ALLY SMOKY CATHEDRAL QUARTZ

Soothing Your Fractured Soul

CATHEDRAL QUARTZ SPEAKS

You are welcomed in, if you dare to enter the threshold of one of my many, vast doorways of light, history, and knowledge—I am Cathedral Quartz. I invite you to know the world in which you live, and all other worlds that have existed. Take caution, it is only brave hearts who dare to witness the glory and the destruction that has existed in the multi-dimensional cosmic territory.

The Library of Congress is like a mini-me, with intelligence tenfold and born of specific Akashic information given me at birth specifically for you. Should you find one of my many brothers and sisters all over the planet, know that we arrived and have been waiting just for you. Our knowledge has been seeded from other galaxies and beings of light.

You might receive me as a bit cold, but once you've hit the age of a hundred million (and I am far older), you've seen quite a bit in life.

You hold those memories in your many translucent planes, memorialized for an eternity. What I am saying is: I know myself.

Truly, this is one of my special gifts: my brilliant, yet detached, persona. So, whatever you may feel, give it all to me. Sincerely, I do not mind if you cry or experience big emotions like anger, rage, or grief. It is a part of your own crystalline structure (lightbody). Your strong emotions are the way you bring the faster reverberations of frequency into your heart and mind, along with the understanding that accompanies them. In my life, I've seen violent storms, powerful earthquakes, and tidal waves beyond belief; I will receive your feelings like a breath of fresh air. When you are with me, those emotions will seem to melt away.

It is your lightbody we have in common. Through the aura (energy body) and energy centers (chakras) that you possess, we communicate. I do this by accessing your passions, for it is the waves of feeling that clear a space for my wisdom. Do not shy away; do not let your instinctual fear repel you from me.

In fact, it is that fear that lets you know I am speaking with you, that I am here, and that you are receiving my vibration by my downloading my information into your being. This is natural and a part of your relaxed, trusting state. I understand that your biology may feel overwhelmed, and breathing deeply helps to relieve the anxiety. Know that you were born a channel, and—by the time you find me— you are ready for activation.

Through new knowledge comes a shift on all levels: physically, mentally, emotionally, and spiritually. You cannot avoid it for it is your birthright and evolution, and everyone on your planet will secure theirs eventually.

What I have for you is a cool and sustainable love you can depend on; yet non-emotional and never-ending. Whatever form of transition you are experiencing, no need to worry, I am familiar. Do not hesitate to access my specific and limitless information to help yourself first and then to assist others. Know that I see what you are made of. I see all you have experienced and know your strength and courage to transmute any apparent obstacle. Never forget I represent the millions of light-beings in the Cosmos who are cheering you on from the wings, and are here to support anything you need, if you'll only ask.

HISTORY

Smoky Cathedral Quartz (sometimes called Lightbrary or Atlantean Temple Quartz) is a unique form of Quartz that doesn't come to an apex with only a few crystalline faces. Cathedral Quartz forms in the shape of castle-like "cathedrals," with many luminous facets and partial points like a stained-glass window. Often the sides of the crystal are filled with etchings and clear "windows and doors;" they truly feel like a small city with winding stairways leading to portals of information. They most often come in Smoky, Clear and Citrine Quartz. Many have been mined in Brazil but can be found within any Quartz cave or quarry.

Today, these "Temples of Light" are less available and tend to be mined or arrive to the market in waves. They are found throughout the globe, mainly in Brazil, Australia, Madagascar, Japan, and in the United States (in Arkansas, New York, and Colorado—to name a few).

Quartz, known as Rock Crystal, is the most abundant mineral on Earth and is a silicon dioxide mineral. They exist in most geological environments and are a component in most rock types. Quartz comes in many varieties including, but not limited to, macrocrystalline (Quartz with visible crystals), microcrystalline Silica (Chalcedony), which itself comes in Agate (translucent), and Jasper (opaque). When Quartz is clear, it is free from other minerals. But there are many varieties of Quartz containing minerals, which causes the different colors available (including Amethyst, Citrine, Smoky Quartz, and Rose Quartz).

There are many Quartz forms or growth types, of which Cathedral Lightbrary is one. In this book you will be (and have been already) exposed to Phantoms, Dendrites, Double Terminated, Tabbies, Twins, Self-Healed's, Agates, and Skeletal Elestial Crystals.

Smoky Quartz, of course, is from the Quartz crystal family, but unlike Clear Quartz, it can be a dark black, to a light brown, to a translucent smoky color. Like its smoky hue implies, it is a calming and grounding stone that helps in processing old habits, history, and trauma.

Smoky Quartz has connections to many cultures and is the national gem of Scotland. You can find it amidst many Celtic legends as it is sacred to the Druids (Celtic priests whose name means "knowers of the oak tree"). Smoky Quartz is also associated with the shadow-self, that within us that remains hidden and is governed by the ancient Greek goddess of the underworld, Hecate.

Smoky Cathedral Lightbraries have been around for hundreds of millions of years, and have surfaced, no doubt, at other turbulent times on our planet like the one we are living through right now. It is a gift from the Earth, helping us to accept ourselves and each other—guiding us to learn to release ourselves from the bondage of certain illusions, such as ownership and superiority, and to expand our universal human culture to collectively recognize that we have a responsibility of stewardship and wellness to both ourselves and the planet that sustains us.

HEALING & SPIRITUAL PROPERTIES

Smoky Cathedral Quartz has many healing and spiritual properties and carries the strengths of both Cathedral Lightbrary formations and the Smoky Quartz hues—it's as versatile of a stone as they come. Its main super-power is to help ground and calm you and your big emotions. It has a wealth of knowledge and will connect you to the hidden realms of your spirit and psyche to reveal what you need to know next. I think of it as a past, present, and future stone.

Smoky Cathedral Quartz are energetic vaults; as you connect to their frequencies, the wisdom of ancient civilizations is revealed. They are a transpersonal stone and work with the collective spirit, in all dimensions of experience: mind, body, and soul. Cathedral Quartz Lightbraries provide humanity with knowledge for spiritual evolution. These crystals contain information and understanding about how we can conceptualize and utilize light energy, beings of light, spirit guides, and interdimensional communication channels in general.

A Cathedral Quartz formation's energy can feel very impersonal— no doubt, a reason they are so effective at calming high emotions. However, the more you work with them, you will attune to their intellectual and high-vibrational spiritual nature. They can be filled with rainbows and engaging stories and help you to access your own. If you are a seeker of multidimensional wisdom and have the desire to uncover the mysteries of this planet and the Cosmos alike, you will love having one of these crystals in your presence.

The Akashic Record is a term referring to a dimension where the memory of all cosmic occurrences is stored, including each human individual lifetime. A Smoky Cathedral Quartz can easily align you with this knowledge, and many crystals are downloaded with specific information to be accessed and channeled by its steward. This stone can impart the value of individualism and developing cooperation within a group dynamic and will show you how others experience life—encouraging you to embrace the perspective of others as you expand your own.

Cathedral Quartz is associated with the crown chakra and time chakra (soul), and with the addition of Smoky Quartz's color, it will align all your chakras from root to crown. A master at balancing your lifeforce energy, there is a biological correspondence which helps to balance the internal environment of the body so that harmful viruses and bacteria cannot survive, and the body can support a positive relationship to pain.

This crystal formation is especially good at helping to transmute and transform cultural trauma. When working with a specific group or intent, this crystal will amplify and harmonize the shared healing field, acting as transmitter and receiver for the collective. When you work with this stone, you will connect to and develop an understanding and acceptance of your value—in addition to your purpose—in this incarnation.

Each of the Cathedral Quartzes (Smoky, Citrine, and Clear) will connect you with different information. For example, the Clear Cathedral Quartz will bring to you knowledge that will mirror who you are and the dynamics and patterns in which you participate, offering you an expanded awareness and choice about how you want to move forward in the world. Citrine Cathedral Quartz connects you to your prosperity consciousness and helps to dispel impoverished patterning. It will reveal the root beliefs that perpetuate your relationship to money and value.

Finally, the Smoky Quartz Cathedral will transmute dense energies physically, mentally, emotionally, and spiritually. It will help guard you from harmful electromagnetic radiation (keep the stone near your tech devices). The crystal acts as an anchor, connecting you to the Earth, and helping you stay focused. Here you'll find your greatest sense of spiritual balance and emotional stability.

Smoky Quartz is a potent transformative stone for expanding awareness in every way you may need it. It works as you work. Additionally, a few things to remember about any Smoky Quartz are: the stone offers security and a sense of stability during times of adversity; it will reinstate a flow of energy to allow the release of physical toxins, emotional traumas, thoughts, and beliefs that no longer serve you or the collective; and it will contribute to the transmutation of spiritual entities that no longer resonate with you.

YOUR CRYSTAL GRID FOR COMMUNITY

Working with a crystal grid is a simple way to begin connecting with the gem and mineral kingdom. You will need the following list of items for this specific grid. You can create a crystal grid by copying the one shown on the following page, on any material you would like: wood, metal, copper, paper, or cloth. Scan the QR Code on page 170 for the free grid download or go here: https://tracee-dunblazier.com/product/your-crystal-allies-the-12-best-gems-and-minerals-for-healing-trauma-and-navigating-change/.

Next, you will create a sacred altar space by cleaning and clearing an area in your homes main room, dining room, or bedroom, on which to place the grid. Write the intention for which you will build your grid by choosing one major cultural issue from which your community suffers, and then writing down your intended claim for what the transformative outcome you would like to create, then place it on the cleared altar space, under the grid. In addition to your grid, you can include a candle, a glass of water, and a form of offering like tobacco, corn, or cornmeal. Now collect the stones listed below and place them on your grid.

This can be an active or passive ritual which means you can sit with your grid for a portion of time daily, weekly, or monthly (with consistency), or you may set up your grid and go about your life in a regular way. The grid works with your subconscious and aligns you to the intention you have set forth. You will receive information in your meditation or mindfully on a daily basis.

> **Smoky Cathedral Quartz** to ground and transmit higher vibrational information to access the timeframe where the community in question achieves your intended outcome. Place the stone in the center of the grid.

> **Sodalite** (six pieces) for calming nerves and communicating authentically. Place in the NE, SE, NW, SW, Center left, and Center Right Positions.

Citrine (five pieces to represent a pentagram) for empowerment, confidence, and trust. Place in the top Center, NE, NW, SE, SW positions of your grid.

NOTES

6
YOUR ALLY DENDRITIC QUARTZ

Voices of the Ancestors

DENDRITIC QUARTZ SPEAKS

Before there were people, there was me. I am the creative life of the party (a crafter); I have fun capturing imprints of plants and minerals that live within the earth, preserved over time and space for all to experience thousands of years later—I am Dendritic Quartz, also know as Garden Quartz. Not everything I hold was born of this planet but ended up here just the same.

My curiosity and fortitude are my most endearing strengths. I am like a manic historian, continually growing, developing, and changing with the times. I can have layer upon layer of different plants and minerals to view—pristine pieces of the Earth's crust on display just for you. Contained in my precious plant medicine is the memory of your ancestors and all they created, produced, and sacrificed so that you may be here today.

I love to help people find their passion. To overcome any spiritual, mental, emotional, or physical blocks that may be obfuscating their view from the deep sense of purpose awaiting them. I have learned over my millennia-long existence the secret to a charmed life: curiosity. It is the one element of every personality that promotes or denies growth, depending on how you nurture it in your mind and heart.

If you continually deny the powerful questions your spirit seeks to answer (for the sake of your survival, for the feelings of another, or to avoid pain), your spirit will become heavy with burden, and your body will become crippled with dysfunction or disease. For it is in those answers that you will find freedom from all your earthly woes. If only you will embrace the spirit of learning and curiosity that you were endowed with at birth, those answers will come. I can help you do just this.

Call on me for simple tasks as well, such as communicating with the plants and animals in your garden. I can help you create an organic awareness of your environment and how other species develop and grow. I can attune you to your true nature and the nature of the Cosmos. All of it, is at the heart of who I am, and I am at the heart of who you are. We are all connected.

In general, I am your all-purpose go-to, for I can mirror your every feeling and transform it from the inside out.

My motto is, "If you're bored, you're boring."

It is my nature to reveal the ways in which you trap yourself and restrict your own freedom. Conversely, I can help you find those elements within yourself again, no matter how long it's been since you've seen them. Here's another bonus: you don't have to trust me, or even have faith. All you need do is show up; that's it, just show up. Don't do it for me or anyone else—show up for you. Trust yourself, and you will find the perfect version of me to accompany you on your road to freedom.

HISTORY

Dendritic Quartz (also called Garden Quartz or Included Quartz) is another branch of the Quartz classification. This variety of Quartz contains inclusions of different plants and minerals such as: Chlorite (white or Green), iron, manganese, hematite Asbestos, and other metallic oxides that grow in a fractal pattern that sometimes resemble ferns. The Greek word "dendron," meaning tree, is the inspiration for the Quartz's name.

Dendritic Quartz is typically clear with white, black, brown, green, and yellow to red fern or tree like inclusions or masses capturing the elements of nature.

This crystal is formed as the Quartz grows over thousands of years and small fractures occur along a horizontal plane within the crystal. The specific included minerals like manganese, iron, or hematite from a neighboring rock or Quartz matrix seeps into the crystal through these fractures. Dendrites can occur in any Quartz formation and is found anywhere one can find Quartz, with the most significant deposits located in Brazil, India, China, Uruguay, and the United States.

HEALING & SPIRITUAL PROPERTIES

Dendritic Quartz is a wonderful all-around versatile stone. It can walk with you on any journey, offering you opportunities to connect to the elemental kingdom and Earth—and all the Divas and spirits that govern them. This stone will help you access past-life information from ancient times, including your relationships to the Cosmos. Dendritic Quartz is an all-over cleanser that stimulates any part of your energy system (aura and chakras) that may require purification.

All Dendritic Quartz create a peaceful environment and support being present in the moment, but each Dendrite will have its own special energy. For example: Chlorite is especially good at reducing and transmuting rage, anger, and frustration. Iron Oxide amplifies the properties of the type of Quartz in which it is included—it will magnify your intention for healing. Hematite is an included mineral that adds a strong protective energy and strengthens your lifeforce energy. A Dendrite with manganese will have "drawing" power. It's a super-manifestor, meaning this stone will help you with your relationship to money and resources; it aligns you with help, unity, and cooperation. Dendritic Quartz assists in expanding your awareness of the higher realms including your own higher self.

Dendritic Quartz naturally shows you where you build emotional walls and set limitations with your own thoughts and belief systems. It can partner with you on your path to self-discovery and behavior modification. It shifts those same dynamics in the physical body by supporting the nervous system, strengthening small capillaries, and re-aligning the spinal column and shoring up the skeletal structure—all by helping one to retain focus, calm, and summon innovative, creative thinking during times of pressure and stress.

In the spiritual realms, Dendritic Quartz is a stone perfect for witches, shamans, and priests, or any other person whose life is focused on these realms and might be traveling between worlds. It alleviates one's fears as they face them head on by offering a new and expanded perspective that reduces the potency of their fear and clears the way for forward movement. Instead of removing obstacles, it helps one move into the blockage to determine its origins and the lessons it contains, so that it may be resolved once and for all.

Dendritic Quartz removes the illusion that exists between the visible and invisible worlds, strengthening one's intuitive abilities. Meditating with this stone will help you to access a new relationship in spirit with those who have crossed over, and for those who may be in the phase of dying. Dendritic Quartz with inclusions will soften the blow that grief can promote. It serves us by opening our hearts and minds to the soul and the omnipotent world it lives in.

Dendritic Quartz Crystal is a powerful healing and energy amplifier. It absorbs, stores, releases, and regulates energy and is excellent at reinstating the dynamic flow of energy in any state or condition. It is the quintessential "start where you are" stone and supports and mirrors what you most need for yourself, at the specific level that is the most beneficial in the moment. It will never push you further than you are prepared to go, but it offers a profound sense of courage to move you to your next level.

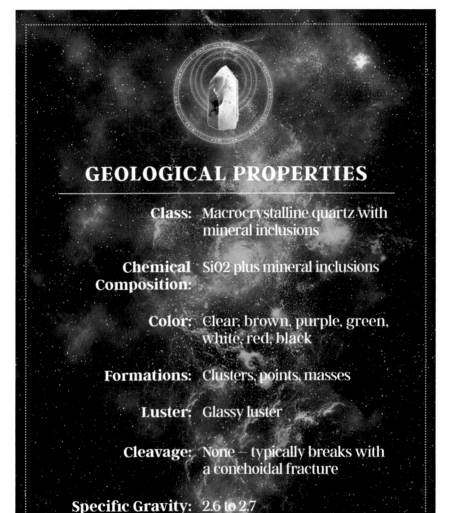

GEOLOGICAL PROPERTIES

Class:	Macrocrystalline quartz with mineral inclusions
Chemical Composition:	SiO_2 plus mineral inclusions
Color:	Clear, brown, purple, green, white, red, black
Formations:	Clusters, points, masses
Luster:	Glassy luster
Cleavage:	None – typically breaks with a conchoidal fracture
Specific Gravity:	2.6 to 2.7
Mohs Hardness:	7

STONES YOU CAN USE INSTEAD: Aventurine, Malachite, Tibetan Quartz, Mongolian Quartz

CARE AND USE

Care of any Quartz crystal is standard, you can soak them in salt-water for a day or two and then clear them during the light of the full Moon, or burn a cleansing herb around their full body, such as sage, cedar, juniper, palo santo, or dragons blood.

You can deepen your connection to Dendritic Quartz by carrying or wearing a stone in your purse, pocket, or on your person. It is excellent as a palm stone, to hold on to in times of anxiety, spiritual seeking, or meditation (when you need to access it for spiritual and emotional support or new beginnings).

Sleeping with a Dendritic Quartz is a wonderful way to take full advantage of all the information the stone carries. Having a dream journal nearby is optimal for writing the details down immediately upon waking from your dreams.

Dendritic Quartz is also a great community stone to use in healings of the collective or to use in the group dynamic. Like any other Quartz, you may set an intention for the group and then use silent meditation or guided visualization to solidify in consciousness the intended outcome for the group. This modality can be used in mass grieving situations to address loss on any level for a group.

MY DENDRITIC QUARTZ STORY

When it comes to healing, we often think of it as linear—the past informing the present and creating the future, allowing for the conscious recognition of trauma we have experienced, and the symptoms it can cause in different aspects of our mind, body, and spirit. We must then consider what we can do to relieve those symptoms. Dendritic Quartz reminds us that that we are one with our imbalances and maladies, and as we change, they change. The conditions in which we find ourselves (our lovers, friends, authorities, and healers) reflect our inner selves on all sides of the spectrum. They inhabit our shadow, and they reveal our light.

To come to terms with such realizations, we grieve; the process of grief is our healing. Over the centuries, this linear view has been a great teacher of understanding the process of self-realization that occurs when we recognize our suffering. Inevitably, it leads us to transmute the underlying imbalance the agony revealed. The Earth is filled with our tears and encapsulated forever in the dendrites that seep into Dendritic Quartz.

I am sure this is why so many specimens of this stone have crossed my path over the years. I notice them everywhere; they are like the mother I never had. Don't get me wrong, I had a lovely mother for most of my life, but an emotional nurturer she was not.

My first carved and polished Dendritic Quartz was given to me as a young girl. It had the traditional fern-like growths inside. I distinctly remember receiving it graciously, loving it in secret, but then judging it somehow. I felt it was interesting but common. It stirred up such vehement duality in the little ten-year-old girl that I was that I didn't offer it much respect or care. It would end up in the bottom of a drawer for months at a time, but somehow made the cut every time I moved (fifteen times over the course of the last few decades). I am not exactly sure where it is today—I suspect in a box in the attic.

Jump to approximately two years into the pandemic (timelines are hard to tell, it seemed like one long continuous year). My favorite gem and mineral warehouse had opened back up for business—I'm not sure why crystals weren't seen as an essential business—and I really wanted to support them. The protocol to visit had changed as external life was opening again to the public: I needed to make an appointment to shop. It took me a week to get in, but I got more excited each day that went by.

Luckily, there was no particular dress code. So, unbrushed hair was thrown up into a pile on the top of my head and clipped in place. I wore no bra, stretch pants, and an XXL tee. I was off to the crystal warehouse! Before quarantining, I did not much care what others thought about me, and that's one of my traits the pandemic strengthened even further. Two years in solitary had erased any sense or need of self-pride. I had spent a few weeks reflecting on it: Do I not care what I look like? Or do I not care what others think?

It occurred to me that I was experiencing some form of middle-aged "rumspringa." I was lapping-up the cool thirst-quenching feeling of not giving a fuck! Of course I cared how I looked, but for the first time, I cared more about how I felt. I wanted to be myself all the time. I didn't want to be worrying about my hair, my clothes, my makeup, my age, my health, other people's opinions, the pandemic, politics, women's rights, black and brown lives, and war; I was done with the "shoulds" of the world. I no longer wanted to worry about things I valued, I only wanted to impact them. And yes, I went out wearing the clothes I slept in, and my smile beamed!

I felt an extraordinary feeling of freedom as I entered the crystal warehouse. As it turned out, the piece I was looking for stopped me in my tracks as I stepped through the door. It was a huge polished Dendritic Quartz point filled with masses of green and white Chlorite phantoms, as beautiful and pristine as the first piece I received all those years ago. But this time, all my voices had been quieted, the judgment and bias had gone—there was only a deep well of gratitude for the presence of this massive beacon of light.

In those moments, standing before this magnificent crystal, I was bearing witness to how much I had changed: how quiet and peaceful was my mind; how open and joyful was my heart; how settled and integrated was my spirit. My body was a little worse for the wear, but it did not matter. I was living how I wanted—a life of integrity that I chose for myself.

Many forms of Dendritic Quartz had walked with me on the path to connecting with and grieving for all my spiritual ancestors, my biological family, my discordant life patterns and deep-seated rage, and most of all the many voices in my head and the judgement that came with them. I now found myself standing there, in front of this massive piece of the Earth's crust, with no shame, no blame, and no tears—only freedom.

I made quick work of the rest of my shopping experience. The warehouse had a crowded clearance corner teeming with deals just for me and even a few giveaways. One of the staff had to help me into my vehicle with my Dendritic Quartz and a few other pieces of crystal, and I was on my way. Now—proudly, consciously, and with full awareness—I headed into my new life of freedom.

CRYSTAL GRID FOR NEW BEGINNINGS

Working with a crystal grid is a simple way to begin connecting with the gem and mineral kingdom. You will need the following list of items for this specific grid. You can create a crystal grid by copying the one shown on the following page, on any material you would like: wood, metal, copper, paper, or cloth. Scan the QR Code on page 170 for the free grid download or go here: https://tracee-dunblazier.com/product/your-crystal-allies-the-12-best-gems-and-minerals-for-healing-trauma-and-navigating-change/.

Next, you will create a sacred altar space by cleaning and clearing an area in any room in your home, on which to place the grid. Write the intention for which you will build your grid and place it on the cleared altar space, under the grid. In addition to your grid, you can include a candle, a glass of water, and a form of offering like tobacco, corn, or cornmeal.

This can be an active or passive ritual which means you can sit with your grid for a portion of time daily, weekly, or monthly (with consistency), or you may set up your grid and go about your life in a regular way. The grid works with your subconscious and aligns you to the intention you have set forth. You will receive information in your meditation or mindfully on a daily basis.

Now collect the stones listed below and place them on your grid.

🪨 **Dendritic Quartz** for starting over with the essence of freedom (five pieces.) Place one in the Center, and then one in the NE, NW, SE, and SW positions.

- **Citrine** for confidence and personal empowerment, placed in the SW position.
- **Rose Quartz** for love and respect of all that has come before this moment and forgiveness, placed in the NE position.
- **Aventurine** for heart healing, prosperity, and courage, placed in SE position.
- **Dumortierite** for connecting to higher inspiration, spirit guides, and angels, placed in the NW position.

NOTES

....

....

....

....

....

....

....

....

....

....

....

....

7
YOUR ALLY KUNZITE

Releasing Pain; Opening to Love

KUNZITE SPEAKS

I am the ultimate get-along stone—my name is Kunzite. I belong anywhere and everywhere. You won't ever feel awkward introducing me to your friends and family. I am just as comfortable camping and catching my own dinner, as I am staying in a five-star hotel and going to a formal affair. I have never met a soul whom I did not love and who did not love me back. No matter how you are feeling, when I'm around, a smile will surely find its way to your lips.

Your people think of me as a young stone because I was only discovered in the early 1900s, but of course I've been here much longer, waiting for the right time to share my voluminous energy with the world! You'll find when you are around me you feel calm. That's because one of the minerals I contain is lithium. Lithium is known for its grounding effect on the brain. It helps with anxiety and running thoughts, and it can help you relax enough to contemplate other responses and options for any trouble you might run across. Lithium can also be found in stones like Lepidolite, Petalite, and Spodumene (to which I am related).

The ultimate love I have to offer you is to lead you gently, consistently, and deliberately to forgiveness. You see, there is only one type of forgiveness but many paths to get there. Some folks learn to forgive themselves at their deepest levels, spiritually accessing the origins and patterns that led to the circumstances they now find themselves in and discovering the seed of accountability that resides within. Others will focus on the ways they have been victimized, finding a road that leads to the forgiveness of the people, places, or things that have betrayed them. Eventually, their attachment to the pain that has been caused will be released.

My motto is: "There is only love."

I will pave the way for you on this divine road to glory through my clarity and presence. You cannot help but feel a little burgeoning joy in your belly when you witness my gold, pink, or purple hues. The subtle pastel colors access a part of your brain and the higher vibrational layer of your aura, where sadness does not exist and there is only wisdom, alignment, and change. I can even make the top of your head tingle.

I can also help with one's relationship to money. My form can sometimes be a beautiful golden brick of light—always radiating prosperity consciousness. Most importantly, I can connect to and transform the physical anchor to the thoughtform of safety. Yes, another one of my super-powers is being carefree. To be prosperous, or even solvent, one must relax and align with the speedier vibration of the universal flow that connects you with the highest and best possibilities for you. When you do so, the concept of choice feels more like trusting yourself and seizing opportunities as they arrive.

Being carefree is not the absence of challenges or worries, it is the presence of safety, courage, and faith to walk through all of them, and I emanate those everywhere I go. I remind your spirit that with an awakened heart your mind and body releases toxins, outdated beliefs, and ideals. They adopt patterns that create new chances for sustenance, joy, productivity, success, and all the worldly benefits that come with these things.

Come, follow my brilliance to a moment of joy, a new perspective, a grand opportunity, or limitless unconditional love. We will start where you are and go from there.

HISTORY

In the rock world, it is customary for a newly found specimen to be named for the geologist who first discovers it. However, Kunzite was discovered by Bernard Hariat, Pedro Fiflet, and Frank Salmons, but is named in honor of George Frederick Kunz (1856-1932), an American mineralogist, gemologist, author, editor, and vice-president of Tiffany and Company. Kunzite is a cousin to Spodumene and presents in many different beautiful pastel shades of gold, pink, and violet. Sometimes, it is irradiated to enhance the color. Many varieties of Spodumene are used in the making of certain medicines, batteries, and ceramics.

I found this interesting clip about Kunzite and its unveiling from 1905.

"The discovery of a new gem is always extremely interesting and scientists throughout the world are always anxious to know the gem's analysis, its various properties and in what form nature has produced her latest novelty. At present the most remarkable gem in which the world generally, and scientists in particular, are interested belongs to California, and was first found about three years ago on a mining concession, owned by Frank A. Salmons, in the Pala mountains of San Diego. It was called 'kunzite' in honor of Dr. George F. Kunz, who is widely known as an authority on precious stones.

"Bernard Hariat, Pedro Fiflet, and Frank Salmons, discoverers and owners of Pala Kunzite Mine in San Diego County, California— the only deposit of its kind in the world.

The comparatively recent discovery of large deposits of lepidolite, amblygonite and tourmaline in the Pala mountains leads mining experts to believe that undoubtedly other rich minerals will be found there. This range lies within easy walking distance of the one-time famous mission which the government has lately converted into an Indian reservation and may be reached easily by train and wagon road from Oceanside."[3]

---

3   Gross, 1905

Today, mines can be found all over the globe: in North America, South America, Africa, Western Europe, and Australia. But in those first days of discovery, it appeared to be extremely rare, and because of its clarity and magnificent hues, it was a much sought-after stone by jewelers all over the world. It was often compared to diamonds and carried a comparable value. After its American discovery, notable owners of exquisite specimens of Kunzite were Tiffany & Company, J. Pierpont Morgan, U.S. Grant, Jr., Governor Pardee of California, the American Museum of Natural History, and the British Museum. Sotheby's auction house sold a forty-seven-carat gem once owned by Jacqueline Kennedy Onassis for $410,000.

The demand for and popularity of Kunzite was because of the large, clear masses of the stone that could be easily cut into gem quality pieces and fashioned into jewelry that was hard enough to be worn freely and become a statement of prosperity for the wearer. The most current supply of this gemstone comes from the Middle East.

HEALING AND SPIRITUAL PROPERTIES

Restoration   Joy   Resourceful   Love
Compassion   Energy   Flow   Prosperity   Harmony

Kunzite is a beacon of love. It is considered to be in alignment with the master number 444, which is the portal to divine love and compassion. It will help you access your divinity on all levels: your body (through the heart); your mind (through the Pineal gland and your sixth chakra of intuition); and your spirit (through the seventh ray of light and your crown chakra). Think about your energy expanding and drawing down your higher frequencies into your body, rather than your spirit ascending to receive or achieve its divine state. This is what Kunzite does.

Kunzite amplifies your ability to give and receive love on all levels and allows you to slow down your mental process when it comes to analyzing relationships of any sort. It has a natural calming effect inspired by the lithium it contains, which will support your management of anxiety and intense emotion during times of trouble, trauma, and transition.

Kunzite activates and connects the heart and crown chakra. This element stimulates your ability to witness higher wisdom and understanding, and then to apply them to any situation.

Placing a piece of Kunzite on your altar will generate calming energy for the entire household. Each color will support different dynamics such as gold for prosperity consciousness, pink for love and relationships, and violet for connections and communications to the other spiritual realms.

This stone will encourage you to let go of your fears and worries about the future, and it will ease your anxiety and confusion in the present. The energy of Kunzite helps you keep your "eye on the prize," so as to not get caught up in other people's opinions, flights of fancy, or staying too long in the future or past. The clarity of the Spodumene variety influences your access to the insights about your history that can help you resolve past dynamics and shed old ideas and behavior so that you may be more present.

It can boost your confidence to bond with new friends and colleagues by shifting the desire to compare yourself to others— to seeking the truth and understanding about what others are going through. This skillset is a specific vibration of empathy and compassion that must be practiced to be fully known, and it can restore your self-trust and motivate your acceptance of others as they are. Kunzite is a wonderful crystal to help you round out all the rough edges in your life, no matter where you begin.

GEOLOGICAL PROPERTIES

Class: Lithium aluminum silicate (spodumene)

Chemical Composition: LiAl (Si2O6)

Color: Pink to violet, gold

Formations: Striated masses

Luster: Vitreous

Cleavage: Perfect, prismatic (Prismatic cleavage occurs when there are two cleavage planes in a crystal.)

Specific Gravity: 3.15 - 3.21

Mohs Hardness: 6.5

STONES YOU CAN USE INSTEAD:
Lepidolite, Spodumene, Rainbow Moonstone

CARE AND USE

It's important to keep Kunzite out of direct sunlight for any long periods of time as its color may fade. It is excellent to wear in any form of jewelry but may crack if hit hard enough, so you'll want to be careful. To clean Kunzite, use a soft cloth along with soapy water, but it's best to avoid harsh chemicals, ultrasonic cleaners, or steam.

It is recommended to store Kunzite jewelry in its own soft environment, so the stone won't get scratched by other pieces. However, the raw stone is very hardy and durable except if it's dropped from an extreme height. Its formation makes it prone to splitting along the prismatic planes of the crystal and will split a larger piece into smaller pieces of similar size, at least that's my experience.

To spiritually cleanse your stone, you can use the light of the full Moon or the smoke of sage, palo santo, juniper, cedar, or sweet grass.

Kunzite, of course, is beautiful to wear and carry, but also a wonderful stone to use in body layouts or meditation grids. It's energy naturally harmonizes with any other crystal that accompanies it. I have worked with my Kunzite many times in guided visualizations for access to spirit guide and angelic communication. It is a powerful crystal to use in entity release and works well with people who suffer any form of mental illness.

MY KUNZITE STORY

I moved to Los Angeles from New York City somewhat abruptly. Feeling pushed out by the forces that be—not by any one thing in particular, but more accurately by a perfect storm of circumstances—I was experiencing a deep vulnerability. I was struggling to transcend the rage that had been fueling my existence for a decade, and I was searching for a way to let love be my guide and protector.

At the time, a bunch of young men in my neighborhood, for sport, had taken to chasing me into my building several nights a week as I arrived home in the wee hours of the morning from my waitressing job. Meanwhile, the foundation that barely held up the relationship I'd been in for the previous year was shaky at best. There, in New York, I was slowly but surely losing faith that something more satisfying and valuable would take shape.

I was given the choice to move to Los Angeles with my boyfriend or stay in New York in a life that was showing clear signs of ripping at the seams. So, I chose Los Angeles. I am sure you can write the next portion of the story: the relationship was not working out; I didn't have a place to live; I was grappling with a deep, hormonal depression; and I was stymied by the complete shift in available jobs in California. The complex process it took to land an available work opportunity was prohibitive of finding one.

In New York City, you could walk into any restaurant, and if they had a bartender or server vacancy and you could prove your experience, you'd be invited in on a trial basis; in Los Angeles, you could be asked in for a myriad of interviews over a few months just for a part-time job. I felt stifled like no other time in my life.

It wasn't until I was able to break through the extreme self-pity I was feeling, access some medication to balance my hormones, and do the daily work to shift my behavior and selfish emotional focus—that things began to change. Although I loved my boyfriend, our relationship was held together by a thin string of my unrelenting attachment, more than the freedom that actual love promotes. There was only one way this was going to go.

Fast forward a few years: I had dropped twenty-five pounds; was relationship free; working consistently; and had found a more permanent, stable place to live on my own. I had just begun working as a spiritualist and had taken my first trip to the big Tucson Gem and Mineral show. For me, it was like walking into a fantastical dimension where you were surrounded by tons of Quartz crystal of all forms, and people came in all hues of the rainbow.

With that level of Quartz and other mineral exposure, I was literally transported to different dimensions every night. My dreams were off the charts, and I was having lucid visions during the day in conjunction with some of the crystal specimens. It was as if they were all speaking to me at once and beckoning me here and there. I had never had such an experience with any of the small pieces I owned, no doubt because of the sheer magnitude of power being emanated in one place. I arrived back home a new person, conscious of all my psychic skills now amplified.

Fast forward another year, I had just been introduced to Kunzite via a precious little specimen that was a vivid violet-pink hue. It was such a powerful stone that fit perfectly in my hand. I worked with that stone for about a year when the Tucson and Quartzsite Gem shows came around again. One of my psychic friends from the spiritual shop where we worked was going. Literally, as she was getting in her car to leave to the show, I said, "Hey, get me another piece of Kunzite if you can find it?"

I wasn't really expecting her to find a piece for me, but within a few days, she arrived back at work and walked into my reading room: "I have a surprise for you!"

From her large leather bag, wrapped in a soft cloth, she pulled out a golden brick of Kunzite. It was almost eight inches in length, four-inches wide, and about an inch and a half thick—and she had only spent the 100-dollar budget I'd given her! I was flabbergasted to say the least. Even at that time, that piece should have been several hundred dollars wholesale.

Immediately, just holding the stone, I could feel my throat being activated with a tingly vibration, followed by each chakra (energy center) moving up and down until every single one was in alignment with the vibration of the stone. From that day forward, my magnificent brick of Golden Kunzite has helped me heal my heart, communicate with love, forgive others for who they have been to me and forgive myself for enduring those experiences. It has taught me compassion in the face of extreme trauma and has been the bridge to see myself as a conduit of love to the world through all I do.

CRYSTAL GRID FOR LOVE AND COMPASSION

Working with a crystal grid is a simple way to begin connecting with the gem and mineral kingdom. You will need the following list of items for this specific grid. You can create a crystal grid by copying the one shown on page 91, on any material you would like: wood, metal, copper, paper, or cloth. Scan the QR Code on page 170 for the free grid download or go here: https://traceedunblazier. com/product/your-crystal-allies-the-12-best-gems-and-minerals-for-healing-trauma-and-navigating-change/.

Next, you will create a sacred altar space by cleaning and clearing an area in your homes main room or your bedroom, on which to place the grid. Write the intention for which you will build your grid and place it on the cleared altar space, under the grid. In addition to your grid, you can include a candle, a glass of water, and a form of offering like tobacco, corn, or cornmeal.

This can be an active or passive ritual which means you can sit with your grid for a portion of time daily, weekly, or monthly (with consistency), or you may set up your grid and go about your life in a regular way. The grid works with your subconscious and aligns you to the intention you have set forth. You will receive information in your meditation or mindfully on a daily basis.

Now collect the stones listed below and place them on your grid.

- **Kunzite** for access to the 444 light code vibration (energy of compassion), placed in the center of the grid.

- **Angelite** for spiritual receptivity and trust, placed in the N position of the grid.

- **Celestite** for cosmic connection to spirit guides and angelic beings, placed in the SW position of the grid.

- **Danburite** to increase the heart-brain resonance in order to create a psychic layer of protection and confidence during access to new ideas and wisdom. Place in the SE position of the grid.

Selenite (three 2" to 3" pieces) to clarify thinking and release any anxiety or tension one may have in the experience of meditation, and to harmonize and amplify the communication between all the stones on the grid. Place the long pieces of Selenite in between the center Kunzite and the piece of Angelite, Celestite, and Danburite.

NOTES

NOTES

8
YOUR ALLY PHANTOM QUARTZ

In the Arms of the Ancestors

PHANTOM QUARTZ SPEAKS

I am the Earth's shaman: there is nothing too heavy or too light for me to withstand; everything exists or disappears within the illusion of time. I thrive under pressure, rejoice at new beginnings, and laugh at the adversity of the physical world—I am Phantom Quartz. Yes, I am often perceived as lacking a sense of humor, but that is not true either. Although you cannot see the smile on my face, know that it is there within every layer of mineral laden Quartz in my body.

Don't get me wrong, there is value in taking life seriously, but the concept is meant to help you stay focused on the task at hand, to pay attention to your environment and circumstances (to stay alive), and to recognize your innate force and impact. If you can do all that laughing, then more power to you. It is often the way, however, that the element of humor has been perceived as disrespect or even evil, and the person who delivers it as oblivious or apathetic—because humans must work hard to remember all the things that have brought them to their demise. No matter the detriment—whether it has been a clear path to the death of their bodies, a damaging impact on their culture and growth, or a slow contraction of their spiritual power—humans tend to forget the trauma left behind in their struggles over the centuries.

This is where I come in. I serve as a cultural and ancestral reminder of the planet's history buried in the Earth. When you find one of my brethren, know that we are, at the very least, thousands of years old, and possibly millions. For one with such a resumé, I love change and variety. I am born and develop on every continent, and I have become more common as new stores of crystal beings like me have been revealed by the planet.

I am a deeply protective stone. It's not necessarily my goal to spare you your feelings, rather I ground your body, mind, and spirit in the truth. I hold your hand through the objective witnessing of the havoc that other humans have caused, the presence of other Galactic beings on this planet, and the cognizant relationship to the actual impact of your choices and their consequences. Know that I will hold your pain in my hands and always keep you safe, until you are able to cultivate your own sense of security, self-trust, and awareness. Nothing you could do will drive me and my assistance from you.

My motto is, "Life goes on."

If there is one thing I excel at, it is the art of new beginnings. That said, I do have to express one caveat: Do not compare yourself to me. I have had centuries to perfect just one of my inner layers. I grow each crystal point (termination), birthing it from the base until a new mineral comes along to redirect my development. If anything, learn from the pattern I set forth; it is active in you as well. Pay attention to and embrace your inevitable awakening spawned by a word or deed, and your response to its repetition over time. Many lifetimes of habitual repetition of certain responses, beliefs, or behaviors causes you to be born with habits that are out of pace with your circumstances or societal norms.

Equally, it is the same dynamic of cosmic patterns with which you are born that update and redirect the flow of progress for your world and for the planet.

I am the alpha and the omega... Hah! Not really. I was just checking to see if you're paying attention: there is no actual beginning or end. There is only a continuation of life and how you want to live it. Your willingness to change and transform as the world around you does affects everything you do; ultimately, it affects what you desire over time. Know that I trust you to make choices that will serve you first and then serve others. Now, trust me to reveal what you most need to know of your soul's history—how you can embrace its truth, grieve its presence, and modify it so that all will benefit.

HISTORY

Before we jump into Phantom Quartz, I'd like to offer a few basic facts about Quartz in general. The Quartz name is derived from the Saxon word "querklufterz" (cross-vein ore) from the 1500s. It is believed to have been referred to as "crystal" or "rock crystal" going back to its earliest known reference thousands of years ago. The Earth's crust is made up of more than ten percent Quartz crystal, occurring in igneous, metamorphic, and sedimentary rocks.

Principally, there are two groups of Quartz classification, based on the size of the crystals or grains of the variety. The two groups are: crystals that can be seen with the naked eye (macrocrystalline) such as Amethyst, Citrine, and Smoky Quartz; and crystals that are too small to be seen with the naked eye (cryptocrystalline) such as Chalcedony (Agate and Jasper). The color in Smoky Quartz comes from the natural radiation coming off other stones in the area of its formation, and Amethyst and Citrine gain their color from slight amounts of iron present as the crystal forms.

Phantom Quartz (also known as Ghost, Specter or Shadow crystals), are created when a crystal is paused in the process of forming, often due to the lack of its silica feed. During the cessation of growth, minerals such as hematite, iron, chlorite, or goethite from the cave walls, or other crystalline varieties (like Amethyst, Smoky or Milky Quartz) form on the termination and are encapsulated there when the original Quartz crystal resumes its growth. This can happen many times over millions of years. This is what makes working with these amazing specimens so profound. The phantom colors can be white, brown, yellow, orange, gold, red, purple, or pink and all have their own spiritual significance.

HEALING & SPIRITUAL PROPERTIES

| Time | Evolution | Ancestors | New Beginnings |
| New Directions | Endurance | Practicality | Humor |

Phantom Quartz is a powerful master crystal that helps you access information on all levels. If one has found its way to you, no doubt it brings special experiences and downloads you need. This Quartz has a special connection to understanding patterns on the DNA level, and past and future lives. The deeper level of comprehension it supports can add levity, as well as practicality, to any transition you choose to undertake or any that may come up unexpectedly.

The multiple phantom terminations within the crystal connect you to the multidimensional world we live in and can help you access wisdom from your ancestors or conversation with your spirit guides. Additionally, these crystals remember cultural customs and traditions; they can help you access yours from ancient times. These stones contain revelatory stories of extreme endings and abrupt beginnings and can be strong mood stabilizers in times of crisis. You will find a profound vibration of calm emitting from this crystal and a feeling that all is well.

An excellent stone to have available during the birth and death process, Phantom Quartz is perfect for meditation with the intent to access higher realms and mediumship experiences. The crystal is a naturally protective stone and can help you remain grounded during astral travel and while seeking further wisdom from other planets.

Phantom Quartz helps you process energy and understanding from spiritual or emotional trauma, energetically helping you to recognize the path of least resistance to forgiveness. It can also become a strong communication stone as well, when setting boundaries becomes necessary. It soothes anxiety, and it reminds you to breathe deeply and lean into your feelings to access the words that describe them perfectly.

A stone excellent for magical practice and workings, it is a crystal that promotes the Truth (the common ground we all share). Be forewarned, though: it can shift the outcome you intend from your spells and rituals, especially while using it regarding others. This is the rock you want to work with to reveal deception on any level, whether within yourself or the betrayal of others. It strengthens your willingness to see things as they are, not as you wish them to be.

The sacred medicine of the Phantom Quartz shores you up to become a witness to your own life and to take authority over thoughts, ideas, and behaviors that no longer serve you. It can help you reset your biorhythms and sleep patterns to nourish your body and reinforce your immune system. It will also teach you to trust your intuition and cultivate patience with divine timing.

Tibetan Quartz (Black Phantom Quartz) has inclusions of carbon, hematite, and manganese and is a super-attractor excellent for working with group consciousness, collective or cultural trauma, and prosperity consciousness. It helps to transform spiritual attachments, entities, and intrusions one may have collected and of which they are unaware.

Chlorite Phantom Quartz is an inclusion of green or white chlorite (often includes iron) and can be used for stabilizing the physical body. Also excellent for heart and brain resonance and harmonizing with the electromagnetic field of the planet. It helps with giving and receiving healing on all levels.

Cloudy White Phantom Quartz contains clay as its inclusion and looks like a cloudy white or grey phantom. This particular phantom is especially good at clearing emotional energy and recognizing the mental, emotional, and spiritual patterns that created it.

Many other minerals can be included as phantoms in Quartz, and there are other varieties of Quartz like Amethyst, Citrine, and Smoky Quartz that will have phantoms. You will want to take stock of the spiritual healing properties of those varieties of stones and minerals as well, to grasp the full potential of healing power of the stone that finds its way to you.

GEOLOGICAL PROPERTIES

Class: Macrocrystalline quartz with mineral inclusions

Chemical Composition: SiO_2

Color: Clear, white, gray, purple, yellow, brown, black, pink, green, red.

Formations: Quartz points, clusters, Fadens, and Elestials

Luster: Vitreous, transparent to translucent

Cleavage: Typically breaks with a conchoidal fracture

Specific Gravity: 2.6 to 2.7

Mohs Hardness: 7

STONE YOU CAN USE INSTEAD: Hematite, Dog Tooth Calcite, Obsidian, Quartz Scepter or Time Link Crystal

CARE AND USE

Care of any Quartz crystal is standard, you can soak them in saltwater for a day or two and then clear them during the light of the full Moon, several hours in the Sun, or burn a cleansing herb around their full body, such as Sage, Cedar, Juniper, Palo Santo, or Dragons Blood.

A way to deepen your connection to the Phantom Quartz is by carrying or wearing a stone in your purse, pocket, or on your person. You can also hold onto it directly in times of anxiety, spiritual seeking, or meditation when you need to access Phantom Quartz for spiritual and emotional support. Hold on to the stone and use this time to reinforce your connection.

Sleeping with a Phantom Quartz is a wonderful way to take full advantage of all the information the stone carries. Having a dream journal nearby is important for writing the details down immediately upon waking from your dreams. These stones are good for group meditation and community work. They are naturally calibrated for ascension and shadow work.

MY PHANTOM QUARTZ STORY

I love Phantom Quartz and have several in my possession today. Many different Smokies, Clears, Citrines, and included Phantom Quartzes have found their way to me over the years, and I rarely say, "No, you are not for me."

Phantom Quartz has always provided me a profound sense of hope and endurance. A connection to my earthly and cosmic family that grounds my faith in the divinity of my soul's journey. My first trip to the annual Tucson Gem and Mineral show was where I discovered two of the most memorable and consequential stones of my life. But first I should offer a little back-story.

I had been living in Los Angeles for about four years and had struggled mentally, emotionally, and physically through every one of them. I was suffering from an extreme post-partum depression and did not have many close friends, especially ones that could deal with the intensity of my emotions at the time. My psychic skills were abruptly awakening into a deep transition, and I was not sleeping well. Finally, one day before meeting my sister for a drink, I spied a little candle and crystal store tucked in between a bar and a theater near West Hollywood.

I stopped in to see what they had and enjoyed a delightful and humorous conversation with the store's proprietor. She was a woman in her fifties who went by a name other than the one given her at birth, practiced a few different religions, and was suffering from continual psychic attacks from, well, I wasn't exactly sure who. Her appearance was always a little drawn and disheveled, but she was funny as hell. I was strongly drawn to her and the goings on in her store, and I quickly found a piece of Angelite I had to have. Fortunately, as it turned out, it was out of my price range, and I giggled to myself when she offered me a layaway plan, which I quickly accepted (and it was a reason to visit often).

Over the next few months, I would stop by the store to pay down my debt. While there, I made a few new friends and saw that the proprietor was connected to several people in this new psychic community to which I was becoming a part. That little crystal store, with its dichotomy between light and dark magic, prosperity and lack, and companionship and loneliness, was a powerful thing to witness.

After about six months, myself and a woman named Gail had become staples at the crystal store in the evenings, sharing stories with the woman I affectionately call the "Crystal Lady". The Christmas season was upon us, and she had hired Gail and I to help with her brand of homemade candles and to help at the store when needed. I was working another job but made it over in the late afternoons. Sometimes we would be laughing and learning until late into the night.

What I loved most about the Crystal Lady is that she had lived a full life and didn't judge others. She'd had hundreds of sexual partners, many careers, practiced several religions, smoked, drank, and drugged her way into a final redemption of a life in a community who loved her, a store that sustained her, and a will to transcend the multidimensional world in which she lived. She had a little swatch of paper taped next to the deadbolt on the inside of her shop door that described her perfectly. It read, "Welcome to mundania," as you walked out the door and into mainstream society.

Just after that Christmas season is when my Phantom Quartz story begins. The Crystal Lady had hired Gail and I to represent her candle interests at the upcoming Tucson Gem and Mineral show in February. She created a contract for each of us to sign, committing to an hourly wage and other requirements and responsibilities. I didn't pay much attention to it as I was excited about this free opportunity to go to the show, and we were feverishly preparing to load up her VW van for the drive from California to Arizona.

The Crystal Lady was struggling to get everything ready, so I volunteered to make our hotel reservations and put them on my credit card, until we checked out and she would take care of the bill. It all seemed so simple to me.

Immediately upon arriving at the show, the Crystal Lady unloaded Gail and I, and the candles, and headed back to Los Angeles to mind the store. She had made plans for us to share the showroom (which was a hotel room) with a few folks who sold magical incense and oils made by the light of the Moon. Little did I understand that what happens in Tucson definitely does not stay in Tucson. The show started out great. Gail and I got on fine with our showroom mates; they were very knowledgeable and interesting to talk to. Their products were amazing, and they had some fabulous stories to share. About eight hours in (the days were approximately twelve hours of selling time), one of the guys asked if I wanted to go take a look around, and of course I did.

I quickly found a jewelry vendor from whom I purchased the largest necklace I had ever worn. It was a massive and impeccable clear to gray Phantom Quartz, with a few other gemstones in a sterling silver setting attached at the top of the Quartz. I bought a chain to go with it and headed back to the showroom to work. Surprisingly, I was completely unaware of the time and had been gone for about an hour and half. I apologized, and we had a good laugh about how easy it was to "lose time" at a crystal show.

Each day felt longer than the next, and Gail and I were both feeling it. We wondered how we would be able to make it through two full weeks of the boredom and lack of traffic to our room. We'd only sold a few cases of candles and people were not showing any interest in future sales either. Gail and I began to take turns covering the room while the other went on a gem and mineral walkabout.

The next Phantom I found was a Smoky Quartz from the Congo: a deep brown Quartz point that I still have today. It's about twelve inches long and has several Phantoms at its apex. It is also included with iron oxide, giving the side of it a frosty red color and allowing for a little light to shine throughout the body of the crystal. I immediately felt so connected with this stone that I spent some time learning about it from the dealer at the table.

At this point of the show, we were about five days in and really struggling to sell the Crystal Lady's products. It didn't seem as if our showroom mates were doing too well either, and all of us kvetched about it. Little did Gail and I know that the men sharing our showroom had been reporting to the Crystal Lady the state of affairs; however, they excluded the fact that some of the days had turned into twelve-hour workdays for both of us and that Gail and I had been working hard to sell the candles. To this day, I am unsure about what exactly transpired. All I know is, about midway into our stay, one night about three in the morning, the Crystal Lady showed up at our hotel room out of her mind. She was yelling and screaming and awakened several people on our floor. She was barking and hissing (literally) and calling us vulgar names. All the while, she was packing up her VW van with the cases of candles we'd been trying to sell. (Soon enough I would l become clear that she was under demonic attack and influence, although I did not have words for it at the time.)

Once the van was packed, she told us to fuck-off: she wasn't going to pay for the hotel room in which we slept, nor was she going to pay for the salary she committed to (only $4.50 per hour), and we could find our way home on our own. Drowsy, befuddled, and flabbergasted we stood and watched while she drove away as the Sun began to rise. I have to say, as shocking and unexpected as it was, it all made perfect sense. I didn't become friends with her for her stability. Clearly, this needed to be the end of our road.

I wore that beautiful Phantom Quartz into the small-claims court where I had to take her to recover a small portion of the money I invested (but none of the salary she promised). She ended up working some of her magic on Gail, who didn't show up to court to testify on my behalf because she'd had nightmares the whole night before. Interestingly, the Crystal Lady was even more unkempt and a lot less funny that day in court than when we'd first met, and she wound up having to compensate me for all of the money I had spent on her venture. Really, in the end, I was the big winner: I got my perspective set straight, all my money back, took a trip, and found some of the best crystal friends a girl could ever ask for. The only thing I lost was a little time.

CRYSTAL GRID FOR HISTORICAL RECONCILIATION

Working with a crystal grid is a simple way to begin connecting with the gem and mineral kingdom. You will need the following list of items for this specific grid. You can create a crystal grid by copying the one shown on the following page, on any material you would like: wood, metal, copper, paper, or cloth. Scan the QR Code on page 170 for the free grid download or go here: https://tracee-dunblazier.com/product/your-crystal-allies-the-12-best-gems-and-minerals-for-healing-trauma-and-navigating-change/.)

Next, you will create a sacred altar space by cleaning and clearing an area in your homes main room on which to place the grid. Write the intention for which you will build your grid and place it on the cleared altar space, under the grid. In addition to your grid, you can include a candle, a glass of water, and a form of offering like tobacco, corn, or cornmeal.

This can be an active or passive ritual which means you can sit with your grid for a portion of time daily, weekly, or monthly (with consistency), or you may set up your grid and go about your life in a regular way. The grid works with your subconscious and aligns you to the intention you have set forth. You will receive information in your meditation or mindfully on a daily basis.

Now, collect the stones listed below and place them on your grid.

- **Phantom Quartz** of any type for reconciling the past, placed in the center of the grid.

- **Bronzite** (fifteen stones) for calming, establishing clarity, and innovating creative process, to be placed, five in a line, leading from the center to the N, SE, and SW positions.

- **Fluorite** (three pieces) for harmonizing you with any unreconciled truth you may have about yourself, others, or history. Place each Fluorite at the end of each line of Bronzite.

9
YOUR ALLY RELATIONSHIP QUARTZ

Connect to Yourself;
Mirror Your Partner

RELATIONSHIP QUARTZ SPEAKS

Like many in your world, some of us in the crystal kingdom have grown together for life. We have been placed in a cluster or grown with a twin or triplet with whom we will share the millennia together. Additionally, like in your world, sometimes one of us breaks away and becomes separated from the cluster or our beloved—be it by an earthly event or a human hand—but to us, it is of no real consequence. You see, in the world of Quartz, we hold the consciousness of Oneness. We are never alone, and we never lose sight of one another when we are apart. There can be no hardship, only the will of the Creator.

This is the basis of the profound lesson we teach about relationships. Now, unlike humans, we do not have emotion. We amplify it and understand its purpose and wisdom. It is a powerful message bringer and communicator of perception and truth. My friends, we know the Truth; we've seen it. We have actually been here for it and hold its memory in the millions of grains of information from which we are made.

—Wait!—Hello! *I'd* like to say something. I am the other twin. We
don't really have names; we recognize each other as the distinct
vibrations we each have (Tourmalinated Quartz). However, you may
call me Latka if you'd like—it most clearly represents my vibration.
My brother tends to be a bit of a "truth monger." He's very serious.
He can make it seem like we don't ever have pleasure. But like any
family, we poke fun at our habits and impersonate one another
to acknowledge our differences. We could do it all day. However,
one of the really gratifying things we do is transmit messages
from other worlds—the big Cosmos! Wow, that can be exciting
sometimes. I'll be sitting here at night, and I'll feel a transmission,
something brand new that I have not felt before; what a rush.

I am not sure I can do justice in words to the immense exhilaration
I feel when this happens; however, there is no bursting at the seams
because my crystalline structure is made for such an event. It's
one of the ways we can help you metabolize the new information
or circumstances you find yourselves in. We know your nervous
system is in flux, and anxiety and depression are the ways you
expand your depths of perception and reflection. It is impressive,
really: your endocrine system, brain, and biology and their precise
messaging and ability to adapt to light energy like ours. You have
so many moving parts, of all different vibrations, it makes sense
that it takes lifetimes to get to know your body, how to take care of
it, and finally to enjoy all that being human provides.

—Hey! It's me again. I didn't give you my name earlier because I don't
have one, but for the sake of distinction, you can call me Germane.
We are grown with information inside our macrocrystalline structure, and we have an innate awareness and connection to a collective
consciousness (actually, so do you). It is the way we entertain each
other while supporting you.

I know it may seem hard to completely understand what it feels
like to be full of compassion and, at the same time, have no empathy, but I was thinking about an event that took place the other day.
A nearby crystal cracked and fell off a cluster; none of us were sad.
Then, it occurred to me that for you to lose a limb or any part of
yourself, or something you've created, it is very sad—devastating

really. But for us—*boop!*—the crystal breaks off and falls to the ground, and now we have two new beginnings.

The crystal termination on the ground has completed its growth cycle (or will "heal itself" based on its environment). It will now live its life as it is, and the cluster might generate a "healed" crystalline structure (a flattened crystal termination that grows sideways over the broken edge), and it will naturally adjust to its new vibration without the termination—forever sustaining communication with the fallen piece.

That is very astute of Germane! He is rarely contemplative. Yes, we Quartz witness your emotions all the time and do have the ability to mirror them back to you and each other. and that includes your deep emotion and empathy for one another. It is a unique experience. Things like rage or self-pity, they are powerful emotions that change your chemistry and open your heart. At times, we have seen them inspire you to take physical world actions that change your life, some that shorten your process and others that string out the undertaking far longer.

If you'll work with us, we can aid you in accessing the wisdom of your choices, communicate to others what you mean, and help you understand and access the powerful vibration of your emotions—how they work with your body and consciousness, and connect you to your earthly and cosmic family. If there is anyone on the planet that knows how to get along with others, it is us. We really enjoy our interactions with you. So, when you find one of our kind, I hope you'll be as open to them as you have been here today, listening to our story. Don't hesitate to bring your questions or feelings to us; we will help you sort it all out. Serving you is one of our greatest joys!

Until then, I'm Latka.

—Signing off, this has been Germane!

HISTORY

In the world of Quartz, there are multiple formations that occur in every variety, and one of my favorites is a type known in general as a "Relationship Crystal." Specifically, this grouping is comprised of crystals that exhibit "twinning" and "crosses." The differences between, I'll explain below. There are many specifications or laws that define the properties that cause twinning, and these formations can be applied in electronics as a frequency control, in pressure gauges, and in other devices (like the monochromator, an optical instrument which measures the light spectrum).

For our purposes here, I am going to simplify the information as much as possible for recognition purposes in your search for Cross Quartz Crystals, as well as the three main types of Quartz Crystal twinnings: Dauphine Twins, Brazil Twins, and Japan Law Twins.

First, how the twins form is vital. Twinning begins multiple ways, but we will discuss two of them here: transformation twins and growth twins.

A transformation twinning happens when a preexisting crystal undergoes a change due to a shift in temperature or pressure. This often occurs in minerals that have different crystal structures and different symmetry at different temperatures or pressures. When the pressure or temperature is changed, different parts of the crystal arrange in a new symmetrical placement that creates an intergrowth of one or more crystals. When a decrease in temperature occurs during the formation of a Quartz Crystal it can form a Dauphiné or Brazil Twin in this way.

A growth twin occurs when an accident happens during a crystal's growth and a new crystal is added to the face of an already existing crystal (twinning occurs when the new crystal shares lattice points on the face of the existing crystal but is situated differently from the original crystal). These growth twins can be contact twins (partially connected and share a base) like a Japan Law Twin, or penetration twins (the crystal growth is within the main crystal and the two crystals share a body) like Dauphiné and Brazil Quartz.

Dauphiné Twins: Also known as Tantric Twins, Karmic Twins, or Soulmate Quartz. These crystal twins are recognized as two parallel crystals growing together and partially merged. They form as clearly distinct crystals or can be merged to such an extent that they have the same body. One may be wider or taller than the other. Notably, their faces are focused in the same direction.

Brazil Twins: Two individual crystals form together, however, one has a right-handed crystal face (a slanted diamond shaped face that leans toward the right), and the other has a left-handed crystal face (a slanted diamond shaped face that leans toward the left). This means that they are like two crystal points facing away from each other, not in the same direction.

Japan Law Twins: Japan Law Twins share a base, and the terminations grow in opposite directions from one another, having parallel prismatic faces resulting in a "V" formation. These can often occur in a Quartz cluster. In 1829, a German mineralogist, named Weiss, discovered this twin form. It was originally called La Gardette Law Twin as it was discovered in the French city of the same name. The current market name (Japan Law Twin) refers to exceptionally high-end specimens that come out of Japan.

Cross Quartz: A single or double termination crystal that has a second crystal crossing the first and which is attached but not completely penetrated by the other.

HEALING AND SPIRITUAL PROPERTIES

Relationship Crystals are a form of Quartz that assists you in connections and partnerships of all sorts, especially in your relationship with yourself. It helps to streamline and simplify the details of a match, and can help to reveal the underlying mental, emotional, and spiritual dynamics at play in any pairing or group. You can also program these crystals with your specific intent for the relationship at hand. Doing so doesn't mean the exact intent will come to pass; rather, it will force the relationship to reveal the true possibilities that exist or how it may play out.

Cross Crystal Cross Crystals are help-ful in making decisions; they help delineate the options available and clarify which would be most appropriate for all involved. These crystals will teach tolerance for those who hold opposing views or opinions and will encourage empathy and compassion for them and yourself. Seeing from another's point of view allows for a deeper understanding of the way someone thinks and feels about themselves and the world they live in. This crystal also helps to cultivate trust and intuitive abilities.

CROSS CRYSTAL

Relationship Crystals support and teach individuality in marriages, or in partnerships where contracts are involved. They help each indi-vidual define and communicate their needs while aligning with the needs of the whole family or company. Each person can participate in the relationship and pursue their own development while remaining attached to their partner, without limiting either's growth.

Dauphiné or Brazil Twins (also known as Tantric Twins, Karmic Twins, or Soulmate Quartz) will help to bring harmony and balance to relationships by promoting nonjudgement, unity, and acceptance of diversity. Twins bring about clear communication in individuals and groups and facilitate building

DAUPHINE' TWIN

relationships on all levels. They encourage your connection with past-life spiritual contracts and soul patterns that must be acknowledged, worked through, and changed.

BRAZIL TWIN

A Clear Quartz Twin (Dauphiné or Brazil), or Cross Crystal, is a high vibration crystal that heals, teaches, protects, and uplifts its steward. It can open, activate, and balance all chakras, as well as clear and protect the aura. It will amplify the energy of all other stones in its midst and can be programmed through intention. Tantric Twin Quartz can help two people work together to achieve a common goal. They reverberate a cooperative energy to assist the progress of the manifestation process. These crystals encourage the user to be receptive to input from everyone in the group and then mindfully negotiate an action that does the most for the majority of the group.

Japan Law Twins share the same properties as other twin crystals, but also teach about sharing resources, family values, and retaining your individuality within a family or group dynamic. They encourage tolerance for others with whom we work and help us to cultivate compassion and empathy on every level. They are also a good business and negotiation stone. They will support you in communicating your needs and boundaries, and show you how to respect the limitations of others.

JAPAN LAW TWIN

GEOLOGICAL PROPERTIES

Class:	Macrocrystalline quartz
Chemical Composition:	SiO_2
Color:	Clear, white, gray, purple, yellow, brown, black, pink, green, red
Formations:	Clusters and points
Luster:	Vitreous
Cleavage:	None – typically breaks with a conchoidal fracture
Specific Gravity:	2.6 to 2.7
Mohs Hardness:	7

STONES YOU CAN USE INSTEAD: Blue Calcite, Chrysocolla, Rhodochrosite, Rhodonite

CARE AND USE

Care of any Quartz crystal is standard, you can soak them in salt-water for a day or two and then clear them during the light of the full Moon, several hours in the Sun, or burn a cleansing herb around their full body, such as sage, cedar, juniper, palo santo, or dragons blood.

Any type of Relationship Quartz can be utilized in many ways regarding relationships and group dynamics. If you are working through conflict in a partnership, place the crystal between the two parties and take four deep breaths. Decide which partner is going to begin by voicing their concerns. Learning to communicate with an open heart is vital in not taking honest communication personally. Take a few minutes to visualize the energy of your heart-light expanding and allow each person to hold the crystal while they are expressing their feelings.

Meditating with a Twin Quartz Crystal can help partners to recognize the need for individualism within the relationship. To have different interests and ideals is a valuable opportunity to cultivate authentic and divine interest in one another—sharing only the same interests does not always support a harmonious connection.

Cross Crystals may also be used for conflict resolution by people who have a close relationship to one another, like family relationships or business partners. An ideal way to address this dynamic is to create a sacred space (altar) in the home or office where this crystal is to be placed with a piece of paper underneath, inscribed with the partners' intentions for their relationship, or resolution to the issue at hand. This ritual aligns everyone involved on an energetic and emotional level to access what they need out of the situation, and what they have to contribute to the circumstances at play.

Knowledge is power in any relationship. Using any of the forms of Relationship Quartz, you can recognize mental, emotional, spiritual, and behavioral patterns that are the cause of the condition you find yourself or your relationship in. This understanding is the first building block in restructuring any pattern or connection that no longer suits you.

MY RELATIONSHIP QUARTZ STORY

Over my lifetime of crystal gazing, scrying, and dreaming, relationships have been at the heart of it—no doubt because of my powerful partnership karma. My spirit came into this life with a deep and abiding historical pain left from past lifetimes of slavery, sex trafficking, abuse, and drug addiction. What that looks like is a baby born with chronic nightmares, demonic visitation, and deep-rooted inconsolable grief. Before eighteen, I cried myself to sleep almost every night; yet, sleep for me was a double-edged sword. At times, my nights were filled with horrid nightmares whose terror consumed me, but there were other nights where I was swept into the arms of beautiful and powerful angels of light that protected me as I slumbered.

After eighteen, literally by just a few days, I was raped. After, out of the many unfavorable options I had, I decided not to press charges against my perpetrator and instead moved from my childhood home to begin the enduring process of addressing the portal of grief that had been triggered by such an event. Yes, there was pain and betrayal in the wake of the sexual assault, but the lifetimes of pain and rage it awakened in me was beyond my ability to tolerate. I moved to New York City in hopes of finding the emotional and spiritual support I needed, which was not available to me in Albuquerque.

Thus began the long parade of glorious Twins and Cross Crystals to come my way. I've been the guardian of more than I can possibly remember today, and currently I have about twenty in my collection. In the early days, it was often the Smoky Quartz Crosses that found their way to me—master crystals that held the wisdom and force to quell my unruly, violent anger. I still own one from those days in New York City, it's a dark brown-black Smoky Cross from the mine in Lincoln New Mexico. I carried it in my train bag day in and day out. It kept me company on the long walks I took, crying for a hundred blocks or more until my spirit was finally quiet. At home, I'd place it on my altar at night with some selenite to clear its ancient molecules.

My favorite over the years was a huge cloudy white and clear Quartz Japan Law Twin I'd found at a show. It was a fantastic joyful vibration that had two heavy, large crystal terminations shooting up in opposite directions. The terminations were about ten inches in length; I felt honored it found me. I worked with that stone for years. It saw me through more relationships than I can count, and it helped cultivate my ability to communicate my truth in a peaceful way.

Shortly after I'd been working as a spiritual medium, I became an Usui Shiki Ryoho Reiki Master Teacher and was teaching my first class in which one of the students, Beth, fell in love with the Quartz Twin. She offered to buy it from me for four times what I paid for it, and after meditating with it, within a few days I accepted her offer. I was excited for her and the work she would do with the amazing specimen.

Flash forward about five years: I'd lost track of Beth as she had moved out of state. Evidently, unbeknown to me, on her way out of town she sold her entire collection of gems and minerals to a good friend who was just opening a crystal store of his own. It was an elegant little shop down in Redondo Beach that a friend had told me about. I was excited to go!

Finally, almost a year later, I was visiting another friend for lunch, when I saw this enticing little storefront with a huge Buddha in the window. I popped in before my parking meter ran out of time. Upon walking in, the proprietor said hello. He seemed familiar but I couldn't place why. His Sacred Stone Gallery was immaculate, organized, and rich with charm and a quaint little meditation garden out back. It had a lively fountain and a birdbath, complete with several magnificent statues representing all the major religions and many animal totems. He offered me some tea, and I sat there enjoying the sunny day and an interesting conversation with him.

It wasn't until I was on my way out that I was stopped in my tracks by this huge Japan Law Twin in a lovely, well-lit glass case. I sat and stared at it a moment and then realized where I remembered the storeowner from: Beth! I had met him briefly many years ago with my student Beth, on the day I sold her that Japan Law Twin. And it was the same Twin in his case! (The Japan Law Twin I'd sold Beth all those years ago.) I ended up staying another hour, chatting with him about the crystals, and left with the twin again.

Incidentally, his price was so low that even after buying it back from him and owning it twice, I still made money. Which, incidentally, was another of the many lessons this stone taught me—how to make and receive money. This had been a lifelong struggle that highlighted my difficulty with attachment and change.

The final piece of this story? There is no getting around it: approximately six months after bringing my Twin Crystal home for a second time, she fell off the altar where she sat (still a complete mystery how) and broke into two, almost equal, pieces. One I kept; the other I gifted to a friend.

CRYSTAL GRID FOR PARTNERSHIP

Working with a crystal grid is a simple way to begin connecting with the gem and mineral kingdom. You will need the following list of items for this specific grid. You can create a crystal grid by copying the one shown on page 121, on any material you would like: wood, metal, copper, paper, or cloth. Scan the QR Code on page 170 for the free grid download or go here: https://traceedunblazier. com/product/your-crystal-allies-the-12-best-gems-and-minerals-for-healing-trauma-and-navigating-change/.

Next, you will create a sacred altar space by cleaning and clearing an area in your homes main room or your bedroom, on which to place the grid. Write the intention for which you will build your grid and place it on the cleared altar space, under the grid. In addition to your grid, you can include a candle, a glass of water, and a form of offering like tobacco, corn, or cornmeal.

I find the best way to work with a Twin or Cross Crystal is to get to know it first—its information and vibration—before bringing any other stone into the mix. So, for this grid, you'll only be working with your Relationship Crystal. On a piece of paper, write out your intention of what you would like to work through, with yourself or another relationship, and place it under the grid.

This can be an active or passive ritual which means you can sit with your grid for a portion of time daily, weekly, or monthly (with consistency), or you may set up your grid and go about your life in a regular way. The grid works with your subconscious and aligns you to the intention you have set forth. You will receive information in your meditation or mindfully on a daily basis.

🪨 **Relationship Crystal** of your preference, placed in the center of the grid.

NOTES

NOTES

10
YOUR ALLY
ROSE QUARTZ

Smooth the Rough Edges with Love

ROSE QUARTZ SPEAKS

Hi! My name is Rose Quartz, but you can call me Rosie. Among the humans, I am by far the most well-known of my Quartz family. By nature, I am a born leader. Being popular is one thing but understanding your value and influence on others is another. This is the main message I broadcast: we all impact those around us in elusive and obvious ways with the love we carry inside. My vibrant pink tones with white ribbons running through them is my hallmark. Their soft and subtle appearance can be very disarming and, for some, misleading. They don't see the power I generate coming, until I have arrived!

I am nothing if not truthful; you can trust me with all your secrets—I won't tell a soul. I recognize how important our integrity is, I mean, doing what we say and being honest about what we do. We build everything in our lives on the little, seemingly unimportant, decisions we make. My specialty is bringing into your consciousness, in a gentle way, what those decisions mean regarding the necessary truths about your value—and the value of all creatures, large and small.

My motto is, "You are right on time."

I am deeply telepathic, so don't worry if you do not yet have the words to tell your story. I help connect your heart and throat chakras so that you can connect your deep emotions with your inner compassion and begin to communicate your most profound feelings in a calm and fluid way. Of course, I naturally disarm anger and other intense emotions, but I mostly help you direct your powerful force in a means that serves everyone in the situation. I am unflappable and will show you how to achieve this mastery as well.

I always enjoy a party; whether I am being of service or entertaining friends, it is a favorite pastime. I don't think working for myself or others needs to be a drag. No matter where you spend your hours in the day, your good and joyful attitude about yourself will make or break the experience. The time will flow effortlessly, or it will slow to a proverbial halt, just from how relaxed you are in the process. A good attitude goes a long way. And sometimes, accepting where you are is as good as it gets—start there.

Finally, connecting with your inner flow and your outer charm is the all-access pass to the life for which you have been searching. No matter your current condition, I can help you lock on to it. Guilt, shame, and grief are a part of life; they are our innate mastery tools and are meant to help you access the transformative love inside you. They show you where you must begin to take care of yourself (guilt), reveal your hidden powers (shame), and open the floodgates of your emotion and prepare you to receive adoration (grief). Let me partner you on this ride of self-discovery, I promise I'll make it better. When you have lived as long as I have, the one thing I've learned is there is always time to make the changes you want and become the person for whom you have pride, love, and respect.

HISTORY

As far back as our history books go, Rose Quartz has been a revered healing stone and talisman from ancient cultures in the Middle East, Greece, Rome, and the Americas. It's calming vibe was recognized and used as everything from a support for all manner of discordant emotions and dreamtime experiences, to a seal that represents ownership.

Rose Quartz is an abundant variety of Quartz and can be found in Brazil, India, Madagascar, and in South Dakota, North Carolina, and Colorado in the United States, among others. It is most often found in large opaque masses but can also form into rare translucent crystals. The color is the result of included minerals of a pink variety (dumortierite, titanium, manganese, or iron) infused during formation. Of course, it derives its name from the unique pink color (varying from light to dark), which has made it widely sought after for healing stones and wearable pieces alike. You can also find huge pieces in the marketplace that are formed and polished into tables and chairs. It's also known as Pink Quartz, or Hyaline Quartz (from the Greek word "hyalōs," meaning glass).

HEALING & SPIRITUAL PROPERTIES

Love   Compassion   Sustainability   Consistency   Growth   Truth   Revelation

Rose Quartz is a powerfully versatile stone that can be used for practically everything. In particular, it can be used for an anti-inflammatory for the body, a calming agent for the mind, and a comfort and peacemaker for the spirit. Rose Quartz is the perfect stone to include in all your healing crystal grids and body layouts, or to carry close to your body all the time.

Many ailments in the physical body derive from long term inflammation that ultimately challenges the bones, muscles, heart, brain, lungs, and organs until, sometimes, a chronic condition occurs. Rose Quartz can be helpful by itself, or in conjunction with other stones, to change the subtle patterns of stress on a cellular level and (over time) in the DNA. This is not activated necessarily by the physical proximity of the stone but by the shift in consciousness the stone promotes.

Emotionally, Rose Quartz specializes in relationships—on all levels, but most importantly, the one with yourself. If you are not at peace with who you are or the condition you are in, it will prove to be an obstacle for others to be fully accepting of you as well. It's true that one's relationship with the world is derived from their own self-knowledge and self-acceptance; therefore, peace, love, and joy are ours if we believe we deserve them. Rose Quartz will gently lead you to revealing and accepting the hidden truths you carry on every level.

Rose Quartz is not necessarily considered a karmic or ancestral stone but naturally sends waves of light to massage away the layers of fear that hold your spiritually reverberating patterns in place. As this subtle dissolution occurs, one must become aware of the origins of their creation—the people, places, and events that have existed over time and space and have brought you to your current condition. Rose Quartz lets you know that everywhere you've been, everything you've done, and everything you are is part of a Divine order. She broadcasts the message that you are perfect exactly as you are, encouraging you to witness yourself with love and compassion. It is through this lens that you will be able to embrace those things within yourself that may have built a foundation of self-loathing, making changes to them one at a time.

As Rose Quartz is connected to the heart chakra, it is an extraordinary leader in transitioning from relationships, grief, and trauma. She helps you wrap your mind around what is truly best for your well-being. She can let you know how to expand the love in your heart for a relationship and to help you innovate your belief systems and ideas around romantic partnerships and the roles you may have unconsciously given them. As we are in a profound time of cultural transmutation, we have been born to a system that was created in fear and must now be dismantled piece by piece. This requires all of us to rediscover our own personal truths and to reevaluate how inclusive we are in accepting ourselves and others.

Rose Quartz will help you build confidence, divulging your strengths and possibilities while putting your perceived weaknesses into context. This will help you recognize that the areas in your life you deem as weak are really the places where you allow others to unconditionally love you—where you are willing to receive their help. The keystone of all relationships is reciprocity, and when that dynamic is not active, the partnership cannot be strong. Rose Quartz will align you with expressions of warmth, happiness, compassion, understanding, and respect, so that you may learn to give and receive equally in all your connections.

Additionally, Rose Quartz helps with the element of expectations in relationships. It assists you in recognizing your needs and boundaries, as well as areas where you are not able to please yourself and yet expect others to be able to do so. Hypocrisy is a powerful teacher of self-awareness. Rose Quartz supports you in asking yourself: first, how do you meet your own needs; and second, what boundaries do you have in place toward others?

Finally, Rose Quartz helps you to put into perspective the deeper meanings of your strong emotions. She brings insight into the processing of anger, rage, disappointment, devastation, and other intense feelings that are intended to help us break apart old, outdated patterns that no longer serve who we are becoming. Rose Quartz holds the knowledge that once we have fully metabolized these powerful feelings and their messages, their energy dissipates completely, leaving us as masters of our universe. The optimistic, comforting, loving, vibration of Rose Quartz helps with any emotional imbalance—including depression, anxiety, and insomnia.

NOTES

GEOLOGICAL PROPERTIES

Class:	Silicate
Chemical Composition:	SiO2
Color:	Pale to vivid pink
Formations:	Hexagonal crystals, masses
Luster:	Vitreous to waxy, transparent to translucent
Cleavage:	None, breaks with a conchoidal fracture
Specific Gravity:	2.6 to 2.7
Mohs Hardness:	7

STONES YOU CAN USE INSTEAD: Celestite, Carnelian, Angelite, Aventurine, Pink Calcite

CARE AND USE

Care of Rose Quartz crystal is standard, you can soak them in salt-water for a day or two and then clear them during the light of the full Moon, place them in a cloth or plastic bag and bury them in the earth for 24 hours, place them on a selenite charging plate, or burn a cleansing herb around their full body, such as sage, cedar, juniper, palo santo, or dragons blood.

Rose Quartz can be worn in any form of jewelry, placed in any room to anchor a peaceful loving energy, and placed on an altar to imbue the practitioner's intentions to become manifest in integrity and love. It is particularly useful during group healing meditations and can be used to stimulate healing of the body, mind, and spirit.

To harness the force of your Rose Quartz, sit in its proximity and simply relax, take four deep breaths breathing in through the nose and exhaling through the mouth. This allows for the subtle bodies to align with the energy of Rose Quartz, and the mind to calm and focus on being present in the moment. Rose Quartz is readily available in raw, cut, and polished stones, and fashioned into beads to be worn and used as a tool for prayer.

MY ROSE QUARTZ STORY

It certainly was a trip down memory lane when I began to contemplate my own Rose Quartz story. My first exposure to it was when I moved to New York City; I have no memory of it before then. Though, it is one of my longest standing relationships. There have been so many specimens over the years, and I have probably given away or sold more stones than the one hundred (at least) I have stewarded over the years in jewelry, raw stones, palm stones, cut geometric figures, and tumbled rocks. I think I've purchased a piece almost every time I've been to a crystal store, warehouse, or show. I can always use one more.

It has walked me through the most powerful transitions (including grief) over the course of my life, and it has never criticized or judged me for my fears, beliefs, or condition. After being raped at the age of eighteen, it soothed my betrayed heart and quelled the profound karmic rage I carried—showing me how, little by little, to transform its force into useable energy, understanding, and wisdom; reinforcing my own sense of security and love hidden within.

It comforted me through every tumultuous relationship in which I participated, helping me overcome my own negative patterns and releasing me of any self-pity or grudge towards another. Most of all, over the years, it has reaffirmed my own strength and compassion by amplifying the love I have for myself and others, despite what they may have done. Rose Quartz has taught me the effortless way to release myself of judgement and regret and to move forward in dignity and with boundaries.

One of the smallest, yet most memorable pieces I ever carried was a one-and-a-half-inch, nearly translucent, rich pink stone with a cut double-terminated point that had been made into a necklace, with a gem quality diamond-cut piece of moldavite affixed in a silver setting towards the top of the Rose Quartz. It was the only piece of Rose Quartz with that clarity I'd ever owned. I spent more than I had on it and wore it almost every day for the two weeks I had it.

When one night, that stone became my protector.

Here is an excerpt from my book *Conquer Your Karmic Relationships: Heal Spiritual Trauma to Open Your Heart and Restore Your Soul:*[4]

"Allies are often people (or stones) we cross paths with, whom we may or may not cultivate lasting relationships. When we connect with them, they will stand with us giving loving support and guidance. I'd just moved to Los Angeles and was driving home one Friday evening when my car began to stall on the freeway. Luckily, I was near an exit and rolled off as the smoke from my

---

4 Dunblazier, Conquer Your Karmic Relationships: Heal Spiritual Trauma to Open Your Heart and Restore Your Soul (The Demon Slayer's Handbook Series Book 3), 2020

engine drifted upwards from the two cracked gasket heads of my vehicle.

Two guys saw what was happening and pushed my SUV into a parking lot where many young folks had begun their Friday-night hang. I got out of my car to use the pay phone, when I was accosted by three people (a woman with two men standing behind her). They backed me up against a wall just out of the light where others were standing. They were shouting at me, calling me names, and threatening to hurt me. I could see the evidence of long-term drug use, recognized by the subtle chewing motions each of them displayed—caused by excessive use of crack. I was caught off guard, but strangely, I was not as terrified as the situation seemingly warranted.

The group gathering in the parking lot (about fifty people at that point) began to gravitate towards us to watch the commotion. But no one was doing anything to help—just watching. I was in a unique conundrum. Having lived in a drug-infested area of New York City in the '80s, I'd been through many harrowing experiences. But here in Los Angeles, the warrior that I had been, seemed to have vanished—or at least had taken the night off.

I was overwhelmed and frightened. I was shoved up against the wall, with only my Rose Quartz and Moldavite necklace to protect me. Wide-eyed and in shock, I stood there. After several minutes of people just watching this debacle, a young woman named Gloria stepped out of the laundromat next door. She was an imposing woman about eight months pregnant and probably not a day over twenty-two.

Evidently, she knew the three people accosting me by name, and when the crowd parted to let her through, she told them to stop—and they did. As everyone backed away, my Rose Quartz pendant broke in half, and a portion fell to the ground (a phenomena I call taking one for the team: when an object metabolizes the energy of an experience and breaks). My foes and I were acting in concert that day, as a lock and key, brought together by a deep feeling of vulnerability and lack of support. I'd been experiencing it for months—as had they, no doubt."

In addition to Gloria, my ally that day was my beautiful clear pink Rose Quartz. After I thanked Gloria, she suggested I get a tow truck and leave as quickly as possible—which I did. After that experience, I repaired the Rose Quartz for a brief time, until about a week later it fell from my neck and again and broke in two. The message was clear, the stones had done their job. I then cleansed its energy with a soak and Moon shine and passed it on to a client who could benefit from its powerful mojo."

CRYSTAL GRID FOR SELF-LOVE

Working with a crystal grid is a simple way to begin connecting with the gem and mineral kingdom. You will need the following list of items for this specific grid. You can create a crystal grid by copying the one shown on page 135, on any material you would like: wood, metal, copper, paper, or cloth. Scan the QR Code on page 170 for the free grid download or go here: https://traceedunblazier. com/product/your-crystal-allies-the-12-best-gems-and-minerals-for-healing-trauma-and-navigating-change/.

Next, you will create a sacred altar space by cleaning and clearing an area in your home's main room or your bedroom, on which to place the grid. Write the intention for which you will build your grid and place it on the cleared altar space, under the grid. In addition to your grid, you can include a candle, a glass of water, and a form of offering like tobacco, corn, or cornmeal.

This can be an active or passive ritual which means you can sit with your grid for a portion of time daily, weekly, or monthly (with consistency), or you may set up your grid and go about your life in a regular way. The grid works with your subconscious and aligns you to the intention you have set forth. You will receive information in your meditation or mindfully on a daily basis.

Now collect the stones listed below and place them on your grid:

- **Rose Quartz** (six pieces) for self-love, compassion, and self-acceptance, Place a piece on each of the points, excluding the center.

- **Self-Healed Quartz** (of any type) for connection, access to spiritual patterns, amplification of desired intent, and reformation of discordant feelings or behaviors. Place in the center.

NOTES

NOTES

11
YOUR ALLY SELF-HEALED QUARTZ

The Mountain Turns into a River

SELF-HEALED QUARTZ SPEAKS

Simply, I, Self-Healed Quartz, am the true meaning of perseverance. I am the warm blanket on which you lay your weary body once you have left your childhood home. I am the strength you call on when you feel forced out of a circumstance or situation. I am the recovery you seek as you are lying in the hospital. I am the solace you cry for as your heart is breaking. I am going to speak for the collective here—we are all those things. We are also the light bringers of joy, laughter, irony, and inspiration. We are the master healers of the crystal kingdom.

Individually, every member of my family is unique. We come in any variety of Quartz and with any sort of inclusions, some with phantoms and twins. We include everything from large elder points or massive clusters to the smallest of cousins that have been broken off the family compound from which they were born—repairing the crack or wall that has created a divide by growing new smaller crystals in a different pattern on their own.

Like you, our response is written in our DNA, but it still takes our innovation, ingenuity, and willpower to overcome, over time, any obstacle. That is the key, to persevere. Take me (us) for example, at the moment there are three crystal terminations on me, but at first it was just me and a beautifully shaped, flat piece of the wall on which I was growing. It cracked off during an earthquake, and you'd think we would be scared—but we weren't, not really. We fell to the cavern floor with barely a scratch, and that is when the new growth began. Right away!

I don't experience time like most humans. I mean, I am thousands of years old, and it took many of those to grow my own surface. Somewhere in that time, a new little crystal began to form at my side. It was beautiful and not shaped like the rest. Based on our position, the new crystal had to be innovative. Now, it has this perfectly flat surface; in another circumstance it might have grown to a point. It also has a little crystal eye in the center of it, like another crystal dropped in from a whole separate piece, and she has enveloped it in love and crystal.

We are masters of the pivot.

My motto is: "When life changes, we change too".

I think what makes us different from you is we don't feel bad for our situation. Humans have feelings that help them understand their condition more deeply so that they may know themselves and their true nature. We only broadcast or mirror those emotions; it is the only way we experience them. We do not have them in the many forward movements of our growth. For example, when we break, we do not feel broken.

I am young, by comparison to many of my compadres, about 60,000 years old. So, I don't want to speak out of turn, but if there is anything else I could say on behalf of the others, it is that we can teach you how to trust your own divine nature. We are all different forms of the same material, growing and moving forward, guided by the circumstances we find ourselves in. We are given one body, and you are given many. It is on the soul level that we can share all our information with you.

Just having one of us in your presence often becomes the time link you need to access not only that part of your story, but your divinity (where the template exists of your beautiful future), your healing, your resurrection, and your next moment. Your job is to be present; our job is to be a bridge for you to your own inner wisdom and healer. Mostly, to teach you to embrace your emotions and the valuable messages they bring. Trust us, and trust yourself. You are exactly where you need to be in this moment.

HISTORY

Self-Healed Quartz has been here far longer than our history books; it can be found anywhere on the planet and can be employed for multiple uses. The different types include: self-healed bases, self-healed termination faces, and Earthquake Self-Healed Quartz Crystals. A self-healed crystal is a piece of Quartz that endured the unique experience of somehow breaking away from the matrix on which it grew. This break can be just a crack or a permanent departure, either way, it continues to grow. When this Quartz self-heals, at the base where the divide has been created, they grow a new crystal shape, sometimes flat and horizontal across the bottom, or sometimes with many slanted points.

Always in a self-healed crystal, one side has a crystal termination (not always at a point, as it depends on its growth environment). They can also be found with a flat termination, as in an Elestial Quartz whose crystals grow flat across a space. The base can also form what are called etchings. An etching is a smoothed area whose flattened markings look deliberate, not as the base would have looked being freshly broken apart.

A Quartz that self-heals does so because of damage to a portion of one of its faces or body and the presence of a silica feed. For example, if a rock smashes a face of a Quartz point while falling downward, the Quartz can eventually become self-healed. The crystals either heal themselves with a crystalline finish or an etched surface.

Earthquake Self-Healed Quartz Crystals are most often found in clusters and have endured seismic activity. For example, an entire

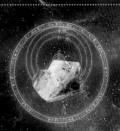

GEOLOGICAL PROPERTIES

Class: Macrocrystalline quartz

Chemical Composition: SiO2

Color: Clear, white, gray, purple, yellow, brown, black, pink, green, red.

Formations: Small crystal terminations, flat or slanted terminations growing across a space, or etching on the broken surface

Luster: Vitreous, transparent to translucent

Cleavage: None

Specific Gravity: 2.6 to 2.7

Mohs Hardness: 7

STONES TO USE INSTEAD: Quartz Point, Malachite, Tabby Quartz, Skeleton Quartz

CARE AND USE

The uses of Self-Healed Quartz are endless, everything from meditation to dreaming to elixirs. An elixir is made with water or other beverage that has been steeped with a stone. The liquid takes on the energetic properties of the gem or mineral and you can take it daily as a part of your healing ritual. Meditation with this stone can promote astral travel and psychic visioning, allowing you to visualize any obstacle that must be overcome to find balance.

Sleeping with a self-healed stone in your bed or on your nightstand can help by inspiring dreams from spirit guides, ancestors, and the higher self, offering one to witness the heart of the matter in a dream state. Also, using this stone within your crystal grid can help all the stones harmonize and focus energy where it is most needed, stimulating and inspiring possible resolutions or healing strategies.

Care of any Quartz crystal is standard: you can soak them in salt-water for a day or two and then clear them during the light of the full Moon; or burn a cleansing herb such as sage, cedar, juniper, palo santo, or dragons blood) around their full body.

MY SELF-HEALED QUARTZ STORY

I was first introduced to Self-Healed Quartz while living in New York City. I owned a little palm piece that I kept with me night and day. I didn't know too much about it at the time, but in retrospect, because I was a healer, it made perfect sense that I was drawn to a "self-healing" crystal. I was deeply haunted by both my soul-history and having to deal with a fresh sexual assault; between them, my spiritual and emotional waters were very murky. Every night, I was having heavy dreams of violent rage; every day, I was overcome by overwhelming emotions.

Although, in hindsight, it is interesting to note that despite my manic-depressive emotional cycle and heavy grief, I was very inspired by my new relationships, workplaces, and co-workers—all of them just as haunted as I. It gave me a feeling of safety and protection no matter where I was, any time of the day or night. My New York experiences turned out to be a preamble for what was to come when I made the move to Los Angeles.

In addition to guiding me through my own spiritual shift, Self-Healed Quartz really took center stage as my shamanic work with others began. Every show, warehouse, or metaphysical shop I visited seemed to be pushing these masters of healing towards me. I could not leave any one of those venues without finding a special Self-Healed Quartz to take home. Mostly, they were Smoky and Clear Quartz, in Twin or Cross relationship crystal forms. It was uncanny. These Quartzes, which would aid me with anxiety and relationships over the years, were discovered in those early days of my foraging for crystals in the Universe, making evident the patterns at play in my life, with others, and the Cosmos.

In those early days, as my work as a healer expanded, every day was a new education at the bookstore in which I worked. Books would literally call me to them, and intuitively I would answer the call. If I came upon a new spiritual predicament in a session with a client, my spiritual guides would generously walk me through it in the moment, but shortly after the session, I'd be called to a bookcase where the needed information was waiting.

I discovered *Many Lives, Many Masters* by Brian L. Weiss, M.D., and his series on past-life experiences this way, and also the book entitled: *Spirit Releasement Therapy: A Technique Manual* by William J. Baldwin, D.D.S, PhD., which helped me understand my purpose. This was the first time I'd seen someone put into words, what, intrinsically, I seemed to know. It was the one thing that was the most difficult to share with others, my ability to see, hear, and understand the multidimensional world and all the beings that lived within.

I didn't seem to have a reaction to or fear of lower vibrational entities like demons, discarnates, or other dense constructs created by humanity over the millennia. Somehow, I felt inoculated to them; I was unconsciously well versed in dealing with their presence. As a child, I'd had many demon-generated psychic attacks, and naturally developed the tools to repel, absolve, or transform them—all techniques that rendered them powerless in my world.

However, it's one thing to be chatting with your own critters in waking and sleeping dreams, but another, entirely, to have otherworldly beings speaking to you from across the table, which was happening daily with the client work I was doing. One evening, in particular, a long-time client of mine who was also working as a psychic reader, called on me to take a session with a client she was working with. He was haunted, and she was unnerved. She requested permission from both of us, to be present at this young man's session and we both agreed.

As I remember, it was a cool fall evening and shortly after 6 p.m. when they arrived. The living room to my small 1930s bungalow was quaint, with an L-shaped set of plush, cushy, salmon-colored couches and a coffee table—not to mention a life-sized stuffed bear I had recently purchase from FAO Schwartz, which took the place of a chair in the corner of the room. My client, happily, sat on the floor (backed up against the bear). Her client was to my left on the smaller-of-the-two couches; we'll call him Joseph. He was covered in many tattoos that didn't seem to have any connection or symmetry (which, in itself, told a story), and his spirit was in knots. It was clear that drugs and alcohol were a part of his personal struggle.

He had spent a significant amount of time trying to address his feelings of powerlessness by working in witchcraft and spirit conjuring, which, apparently, had gotten out-of-hand. When one struggles with their own hopelessness, they tend to attract entities and spirits that amplify that powerlessness, which is what was going on here. Joseph sat on the couch, catty-cornered to me, and told me of an entity that had been with him for months. He couldn't sleep or eat, and he was at his wits' end.

At the time, I had a large Self-Healed Smoky Cathedral Lightbrary, which I spoke of in an earlier chapter, sitting on my altar, and another master-healer Self-Healed Clear Quartz in my hand. As we spoke, I could see a large snake-like entity wrapped around him. Joseph was pleading for my compassion and help. All the while, this critter was up to no good, seething and hissing. About twenty minutes in, Joseph started to visibly cry; he got up from his seat and fell to his knees in front of me, placing his weeping face on my lap. The session had gone from strange to stranger: I glanced over at my client, and she was sound-asleep, nuzzled peacefully up to the bear.

As Joseph whimpered and wailed, the entity that accompanied him was saying, "I am going to get inside you. You have no power. Let me in."

I could hear it plain as day. While my following words addressed the grieving man on his knees, I was responding in my mind simultaneously to the critter directly with a forceful, "NO!"

"Joseph, this entity is manipulating you through your emotion, within your grief you will find your power."

The entity was hoping to manipulate me through my empathy and pride, by getting Joseph to genuflect in submission and to appear broken.

All-the-while, my client was still secure in her powernap, this scenario continued for about fifteen minutes. It ended when I told the critter it had no power in this place, and I commanded Joseph to get up off his knees and sit in his space—to take authority over *his* body and *his* energy. It must have sounded like I was scolding him, calling him by his full name, but as I said it, it was like he woke up from a long sleep, slightly disoriented and looking around the room.

He felt refreshed and a bit confused. I explained to him that the entity had come to show him the meaning of power and authority by requiring him to claim it. I also told him, for now, the entity had departed—but he would surely be watching and waiting for another opportunity to be given influence in Joseph's life. He was the only one who could access the origin of the attached entity. At this point, my client was sheepishly awake and wondering what happened. We wrapped up the session and said good night. I never heard from Joseph again.

I was profoundly grateful to be partnered by those two powerful Self-Healed Quartzes that night. They generated safety and confidence and clearly delineated the dynamic at work and the path forward. They showed me how I could set boundaries in the space while not diminishing Joseph in any way, shoring him up and supporting him in his battle for autonomy.

...All while helping my client catch some obviously much-needed Zs.

CRYSTAL GRID FOR HEALING PERSONAL POWER

Working with a crystal grid is a simple way to begin connecting with the gem and mineral kingdom. You will need the following list of items for this specific grid. You can create a crystal grid by copying the one shown on the following page, on any material you would like: wood, metal, copper, paper, or cloth. Scan the QR Code on page 170 for the free grid download or go here: https://tracee-dunblazier.com/product/your-crystal-allies-the-12-best-gems-and-minerals-for-healing-trauma-and-navigating-change/.

Next, you will create a sacred altar space by cleaning and clearing an area in your homes main room or your bedroom, on which to place the grid. Write the intention for which you will build your grid and place it on the cleared altar space, under the grid. In addition to your grid, you can include a candle, a glass of water, and a form of offering like tobacco, corn, or cornmeal.

This can be an active or passive ritual which means you can sit with your grid for a portion of time daily, weekly, or monthly (with consistency), or you may set up your grid and go about your life in a regular way. The grid works with your subconscious and aligns you to the intention you have set forth. You will receive information in your meditation or mindfully on a daily basis.

Now, collect the stones listed below and place them on your grid.

- **Self-Healed Quartz** to access the healing field, placed in the center of the grid.
- **Black Tourmaline** (four pieces) for power, protection, and grounding, placed in the N, S, E, and W positions.
- **Rhodonite** (four pieces) for stimulating, clearing, and activating the heart chakra and helping to access information about any active emotional wounds, and reconciling them. Place these stones in the NE, SE, NW, SW positions on the grid.
- **Selenite Rods** (four pieces) for removing energetic blocks and balancing and harmonizing all the chakras. Place these stones in between the center and the NE, SE, NW, SW positions.

NOTES

....

....

....

....

....

....

....

....

....

....

....

12
YOUR ALLY ANDARA

Rift of the Past — Wave of the Future

ANDARA SPEAKS

I am the light-bringer to the world, brought here to assist the planet and the beings on it with their multidimensional ascension. Know that you are safe. The Earth and all her inhabitants are going through a shift of the lightbody, which is the way you exist in other times and spaces as well as here. It is what anchors your power in this world. This can mean many things, depending on the viewpoint where you start.

It can mean confidence and self-worth, service, transformation, transmutation, freedom, expansion, and light. For these dynamics are your power and govern the way you attract and manage all your resources. When you find controversy in your discovery of the light, it is the way your biology, your molecules, are awakened. It is the way your heart and mind are awakened. The more you resist the light in your soul system, the more you will reject your goodness. When you move towards your goodness, your light expands. This is the human story over the millennia.

I think it may be best to say, I am the spirit of the light who's found a home in the Andara crystal material (crystal-glass and man-made glass). You see, the glass is only the carrier; I am the light. I am from another time and space with a hand in this one.

The beautiful, multi-colored forms of Andara crystals (what they have come to be known), are not crystals in the scientific sense, they more closely resemble Obsidian, and the process it goes through to come into existence. A mixture of heat, pressure, sand, metal, and minerals. Although Andaras are not of volcanic origins, they are like a cross between glass, Obsidian, Moldavite, and Tektite. Today, all five can be considered in the same family of materials, all with fifth-dimensional access and properties.

Every representation of love is light, and light is love. I connect you to that Truth. The more you release fear, the more you can recognize your power and experience its freedom.

"Freedom is life," is my motto—no more, no less.

There are many dimensions of existence and understanding. You live in the Third Dimension of physicality, you see spiritually in the Fourth Dimension, and you hear energy in the Fifth Dimension. When you practice and heighten your faster vibrating skills of clairsentience (channeling or accessing information intuitively and telepathically), clairaudience (to hear energy and words that may be thought but are not physically spoken), and clairvoyance (to see spirit and other matter in your mind's eye in its perfection), you begin to understand the light codes on which your planet and your body are built, and their relationship to all other things.

When you look into my beautiful crystal-glass you will be drawn into worlds of wonder. Everything is a representation of light—any object that can be seen is viewed only because light from that object travels to our eyes. As you look at any object, you can see it because it is illuminated with light, and that light reflects off it and travels to your eye. This is a basic understanding of physical perception. Now accelerate that idea to not only your vision, but your hearing, understanding, and beyond. The more information to which you are open—the more you exert your will to overcome your natural resistance to the amplification of your light—the more your inner sight will become an outer experience, and you will be free to travel the multiverse.

I am compelled to give you some examples of this so-called superpower. When you are sick, you may travel to the dimension where your illness began to better understand its purpose in your life, or you can travel to a dimension in the future where you are completely well, to better comprehend steps you can take to get there. This is essentially what you might call magick, but from a linear perspective, it is logic. When you have a 360-degree view of your condition, you are empowered to change it.

That was fun; let's find the magick in another example: relationships. When you are in a relationship and not feeling your love is reciprocated, you can travel to the dimension, past or future, where you alone are happy—then witness if your partner is with you. This will give you three bits of information: why your happiness left, what it takes to get it back, and where your partner is on that continuum. You cannot possibly be in a happy relationship if you do not possess happiness.

As Andara shines its light on you, you shine your light everywhere else. If I call to you, our meeting is inevitable. Move forward fearlessly with grace, fortitude, and openness. I will assist where there are blocks on any level. I will show you the integrated, full spectrum version of you and your world, and reveal to you your goodness.

HISTORY

Andaras begin with sand, minerals, and metals, heated until they form glass. In the sand are tiny grains that are variations of Quartz crystal, hence the name Andara crystals. Natural glass forms in pockets all over the world, in deserts and oceans, places that harbor an extreme heat and then a cool environment and mineral filled quartz sand.

The glass that is referred to as Andara is formed in places where there is evidence of a powder containing single-atom minerals called ORME (Orbitally Rearranged Monatomic Element)—a high-spin, single-atom substance. The torsion it creates relates to the subtle energetic forces believed to lie at the causal level of the energy field—behind the forces of electromagnetism and gravity. The unique composition of this material provides benefits that cannot be accessed in any other state and are known to exhibit quantum physical behaviors such as super fluidity, unexpected responses to gravity, tunneling, and magnetic levitation.[5]

The ORME powder can include monatomic Gold, Silver, Iridium, and Rhodium (to name a few), and it occurs where monatomic gasses have infected the quartz and other minerals in the environment. This natural mineral complex exhibits extraordinary properties that strengthen and stabilize the electromagnetic fields of the human body. These high-vibrating minerals are considered to be exotic matter by science and are not yet fully understood, because they have yet to be fully studied.

The other metaphysical element of Andara crystal-glass, that hasn't yet been proven sufficiently in the scientific community but has been bourgeoning in the metaphysical and spiritual community since ancient times, is the presence of an interdimensional element called Iropya (its channeled name). Its energetic effects are activated in the etheric body of the glass by the combination of the Iridium and Rhodium contained in the Etherium (a specific combination of elements making up the Prima Matre—original matter first arriving here from off-planet sources).

The hidden element, Iropya, is a chemical formula for the essence of freedom that exists in another timeframe, it connects to the etheric body of the many different variations of the Andara material and its relations (including glass, Obsidian, Moldavite, and Tektite). It makes sense there is enormous conflict and contrasting information around Andaras as they require a deep-seated shift in perspective, openness, and trust—not just about the reality of the information they propose, but literally everything. One must

---

5   The Hollistic Science Company, 2022

be willing to relinquish the sense of control they have for the need to delineate, and to be willing to receive larger downloads of information at one time.

I am no different. As I worked with what I will call the "new" Andaras (the one pictured here), I read some information that became too complex for my mind to receive, so I altered my state of consciousness by napping while my right brain was receiving the channeled information necessary to bring all the elements of the story and its expression together at one time. There was a moment when I was asleep, yet I was telling myself it was time to wake and write down the transmission I'd just received. This is an example of life on a smaller scale for all of us: our time is a series of waking, sleeping, and processing on every level. The Andara family personifies this experience.

Andaras can exist anywhere on the planet this chemical composition can be found, currently in the High Sierra mountains (and other places in the U.S.), and Northern and Southern Africa, to name a few. Soon, it will be revealed in many new places on Earth. One of the first to be openly discovered, shared, and studied was a property in Northern California, near Mount Shasta.

Andara Crystals are found in many colors, caused by the metal oxides found in the soil such as Iron, Manganese, Cobalt, Copper, Nickel, Titanium, Gold, Silver, and Uranium. As far as the name Andara, it is a bit of a mystery, and is believed to be channeled by one of the early Andara researchers. You can find Andaras in shops and online, and there is quite a bit of controversy about pricing. In the last several decades there have only been a few places of discovery, and as those resources began to run out, the price per gram went up. Currently, there are more resources available (mostly near diamond mines), and the prices have levelled out. When you find a piece labeled from an original source, the price will be higher. No matter your intent, it is never good medicine to pay more than you want for a healing tool.

As always, with any product, there are costs to excavation, shipping, handling, and distribution to wholesalers—depending at which point you purchase yours will determine the price. The good news: you do not need to be a steward to an Andara to receive the benefits or illumination. If you find one you like, work with a photo of it instead of making a purchase. If you find one and are concerned about its material or provenance, remember that working with any of the Andara family (including glass, Obsidian, Tektite, and Moldavite) will allow you to access the etheric body of an Andara if that is your intent.

HEALING AND SPIRITUAL PROPERTIES

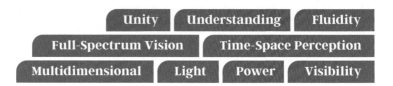

Andara crystals offer a unique experience, unlike any other in the gem and mineral kingdom. They work with your perspective and awareness, can seem to appear and disappear, and can reveal phantoms and other inclusions and patterns in certain lights where at other times they are not apparent. Depending on your current perspective and belief systems, they can draw you in or repel you. It is the reason Andaras are labeled as a fifth-dimensional stone. Every individual works with and responds to the stone's properties starting where they are.

Andara crystals can come in the form of sharp-edged masses, water or sand worn smoothed edges, or they can be cut and polished into shapes. All these forms can serve your particular needs, and do not amplify or diminish their physical or spiritual properties. There are many different colors and hues. Based on those to which you are attracted, the healing ray of the crystal-glass will be focused.

Andaras are teachers of the multidimensional system in which we live. They help to develop your clairsentience, clairaudience, and clairvoyance. The "awakening," as it is called in the healing communities, refers to the physical aspects of your endocrine system during different developmental stages of human life, the energetic awakening of empathy and emotion promoted by the heart and Limbic system, and the mind's ability to perceive and connect to the multiple dimensions of energy, opening it to the Universal Truth governed by our highest level of energy, or Creator. They are tools for profound healing, awakening, and accessing your full potential.

Andaras can assist on all the following levels: body, mind, and spirit.

BODY: Andaras can help you relate to your physical body in a holistic way, by allowing you to see the many individual building blocks and systems of which your body is made. When you have this newly calibrated perspective and detail you are better able to clear blockages and heal yourself. Pain in the body exists as the voice of your physique to your heart and mind for the purpose of communicating stress levels. Accepting pain, and listening to its message, is what helps suffering go away. Andaras will help you receive and understand any messages your body seeks to communicate. Finally, Andaras support your DNA in adapting to your current needs and environment.

MIND: Andaras help to recalibrate the nervous system and all the mental and emotional maladies created by its imbalance, including anxiety and depression. The mind and emotions are strongly connected, and one helps to inform and describe the other. Andaras will help you see the truth of any situation so that you may understand its greater purpose and be able to recognize the actions needed to be taken to shift your experience. When this shift in perception occurs, you experience an increase of your vibration. The faster your thoughts and feelings energetically spin, the more you will release through grief: outdated beliefs, ideas, and emotions. For example: let us take the concept of superiority; it does not apply to consciousness and is only a concept meant to connect possible resolutions with needs. There is no consciousness that is better than another, yet humans continually seek to compare their consciousness to another's, and then label it as inferior or superior.

SPIRIT: Andaras can help clarify the aura of unneeded information and energy; this "awakening" is a series of this type of clearings.

As your energy shifts from these changes of mentality, your body will release any emotions that align with the releasing vibration and the heart will "open." When we say "open heart," we mean that the energy expands to be more inclusive and positive in nature. Your heart chakra (energy center) does actually open, which explains the wide berth of acceptance and connection.

The term "light codes" are a way to describe the different vibrations of the specific light ray's color. We access these light codes when we shift vibrations through changes in thought and perception, through the grief process, and through bringing more light into the physical body with meditation and self-awareness. Andaras will help you to access your own soul-history and the ancient wisdom of the planet.

One of the most powerful attributes of the Andara is to show you a fuller perspective of yourself, others, and the Earth. It is only through this deeper and more magnified understanding that we will learn to love, which is our eternal birthright.

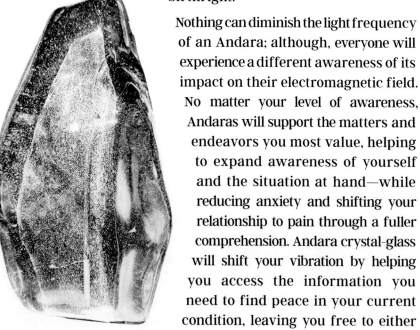

Nothing can diminish the light frequency of an Andara; although, everyone will experience a different awareness of its impact on their electromagnetic field. No matter your level of awareness, Andaras will support the matters and endeavors you most value, helping to expand awareness of yourself and the situation at hand—while reducing anxiety and shifting your relationship to pain through a fuller comprehension. Andara crystal-glass will shift your vibration by helping you access the information you need to find peace in your current condition, leaving you free to either find a resolution or to effortlessly remove the conflict.Andaras are master crystals of feeling change, but in a profoundly instant way.

Although the process of transition may have been in motion for quite some time, this crystal-glass has the ability to quickly remove the obstacles that keep you from accepting and witnessing such transformations. They also support the cultivation of self-honesty, faith, hope, and inspiration. Often, we as humans are partial to self-critique and look at things such as disease and aging as weaknesses to be fixed or healed. Through the lens of an Andara, you will begin to recognize the power and wisdom of every condition and your relationship to it. Not all healing is fixing the physical condition, but all healing requires acceptance of it.

Andara crystals can be found in multiple colors, and each of them have their own additional energies of support. The aqua blue Andara crystal relates to the high-heart chakra or the thymus chakra and opens the pathways for Divine communication and soul connection. This color teaches one to speak from the heart with new levels of honesty and truth. It lessens the need to speak harshly, removing the need to verbalize thoughts which are not in harmony with the essence of the situation. (I can attest to this!)

Andaras will support a shift to a more loving and deliberate communication style. Specifically, the color aqua assists in the recognition of guilt, blame, self-pity and pride, the purpose they serve, and the messages they contain. Andara can help cultivate self-acceptance and a perspective or behavior of worthiness, creating a spiritual integration that allows for fuller receptivity of all positive resources.

GEOLOGICAL PROPERTIES

Class:	Silicate, monatomic glass, volcanic glass
Chemical Composition:	Individual to the specific environment, plus SiO2
Color:	Many Variations of gold, brown, red, pink, green, and blue
Formations:	Masses
Luster:	Vitreous, transparent to translucent
Cleavage:	None
Specific Gravity:	2.20–3.00
Mohs Hardness:	5.5

STONES YOU CAN USE INSTEAD:
Moldavite, Obsidian, Tektite, Glass

CARE AND USE

All crystals and stones may be used similarly, and their care may vary depending on the unique aspects of the stone. Andaras, for a glass material, are fairly hardy but should be respected as you would any other glass item. Because the material is solid, if dropped it most likely will not shatter, but it might leave a shatter imprint as a rock would to the windshield of your car.

Andaras are one of only a few stones that do not need to be energetically cleansed as they transmute and transform the energy around them. They do, however, appreciate a sunlight or moonlight bath and ceremonial smoke.

Whether holding it in your bare hands or having it in your bed is a good idea depends on the size, smoothness, and shape of the piece you steward. The raw, jagged Andara material might better serve you in a thick cloth pouch to carry, or in a prominent place on your altar.

Any small or smoothed specimen can be carried, worn, dreamed with, and held in your hands during meditation. You can use shampoos, window cleaners, or soft bristle brushes to clean an Andara. A good practice to make into a habit is to offer some ritual smoke every time you work with your Andara, or while in prayer or energetically connecting to one of the Andara family.

MY ANDARA STORY

Writing about Andara and its family has been a profound experience for me. I'd only just discovered Andaras six-months prior (or so I thought) and had been studying anything I could find about it—taking interviews with notable people in the historic Andara community, but mostly eating, drinking, sleeping, and dreaming with Andara by my side.

As it turned out, Andara is a trickster and shapeshifter, if you know that medicine; it is a powerful teacher of self-trust, intuition, vision, and self-reliance. The Andara crystal-glass companioned me through the death of my brother-in-law and my sister's grief, the seventeenth anniversary of being in my home and dealing with many major appliance deaths and plumbing issues—always a powerful metaphor, losing water (i.e., resources, emotion)—and the Andara had sat in my presence for more than six weeks before revealing to me the magnificent phantom it carried.

It was about a month after my brother-in-law's death that I went to visit my sister. I brought four small Andara discs to help ease her grief. Her husband's swift and unexpected death from COVID and the abrupt end of their twenty-five-year relationship was unbearable for her. She had never grieved this way, and alone at that.

When I arrived at their newly built home, it was sparsely decorated compared to the organized, antique clutter I am used to in my historic house. Everything was new, clean, and in its place. I shared with her the Andaras by offering her two; I thought that was a good number to start with for someone not into metaphysics in the least, and I knew she would humor me by taking them. Her color choices were either red, sage, green, or opalescent. She picked the red and opal ones, immediately placing them on the side table next to her chair in the living room.

Not giving them another thought, we moved on with the day until several hours later when her anxiety began to rise in the evening, and I suggested she hold the crystals in her hands. As she reached for them, we discovered they were both missing. They had simply disappeared. Neither of us had touched them; despite that, we looked everywhere, and they were nowhere to be found. It was as if they were drawn into a portal to another time and space.

I suggested they'd been drawn into the "portal", and then retrieved the other two from my bag for her. Over the six days we spent together, all of the Andaras would pop up in unusual places where neither of us had put them. The two I had intended to take back home with me, but had given to her that night, disappeared but were found later. After arriving home, I found the green one in my bag, and the sage and red colored ones revealed themselves again next to her chair—the third opalescent crystal is still in the "portal."

Despite the deep grief she was living in, we laughed several times a day with the Andaras "magically" going in and out of sight. It helped her feel connected to her husband and recognize the multidimensionality of the world we live in, to which she became unwittingly exposed through the Andaras.

As for me, I have always had awareness of my spiritual sight, but struggled with intense karmic rage in my younger years that has now transformed into subtle, patterned outbursts of frustration at times of unfortunate surprise. I have greatly exercised these patterns in the last several months during the breakdown of many major appliances, in addition to gas and plumbing leaks during our extreme California drought where the consequences are dire, environmentally and civically. In my heart, I am at peace knowing that eventually all will be well and taken care of, but my brain still has the hair-trigger response of feeling frustrated and defeated, which makes me want to curse, to release the stress.

Enter Andara. I had just received my first shipment of a few pieces and had been working with one in particular (pictured here), when I found water running down my brand-new brick-designed driveway, part of the complete restoration of my 1907 Victorian Bungalow for which I had been saving for years. At first, I told myself it was just a sprinkler line, and I didn't have my normal frustrated reaction. I found a way to turn the water off when it took a few days to get a plumber to come look. Still no anger or frustration peeking out. Finally, at the diagnosis of a broken main waterline directly under my beautiful brick driveway that would now need to be dug up, I responded coolly, with the ease of a building contractor, "Anything that can be built can be rebuilt with a little cash." Even with the thirty-percent pandemic markup, still, I had not even an itty-bitty outburst of emotion.

Who was this person? I thought to myself. What is different in this scenario? It was the Andaras in my space. They seemed to imbue my home, and my brain, with a sense of inspiration and hopefulness.

My strange, immediate responses were ones of freedom and grati-tude. Better now than later, I thought.

Shortly, after this experience, I was sitting in my writing chair, with the large turquoise Andara at my side—as the bright afternoon light shone directly through it. This was not the first time I'd seen the pre-evening light make contact with the crystal, but on this day, for the first time, there was an incredible phantom. Its shape reminded me of Mother Mary and the powerful sense of calm that comes with knowing you are being taken care of in obvious and hidden ways. This stone had been in my home for at least six weeks, and this was the first time the phantom was revealed. As it turns out, each of the Andaras, for which I am the current guardian, have revealed magnificent phantoms; one just yesterday, as I was writing this chapter.

Truly, the communication between me and the Andaras is fantas-tical and, for someone who has had many profound spiritual and para-normal experiences, slightly unexpected. It showed me a powerful Truth about the Fifth Dimension and our inevitable global shift to a deeper understanding of our world, ourselves, and each other. The Truth was about peace, kindness, and surprise.

As people transition into a less rigid knowing and wisdom, for some, there tends to appear a subtle arrogance in the languaging of describing what it means to ascend. A better-than-you implication, if you will, that always inspires a bit of disappointment when I see it. I recently sat on a panel where a panelist shouted at the audience, "Glass is 5D, not plastic!" What she meant was when adjusting to concepts of the Fifth Dimension the idea is that there is a raise in vibration to elements that can be sustainable by everyone includ-ing the planet. It is with that sentiment that the woman engaged the audience in her frustration. My gut reaction was to laugh. What is she doing? I thought. She seemed so angry the entire time.

Then of course, I realized I shared the same pattern of frustration at so-called inanimate objects and the dynamic of surprise, which brings me to the origin of my Andara story. It began many years ago with Moldavite. The asteroid glass is not exactly the same, but it has a connection to the multidimensional time-space-perspective properties as the Andara crystal-glass does, and the experience is even a little more abrupt and shocking of a vibration.

Over the last thirty years I have procured and stewarded more than twenty pieces of Moldavite, and within weeks of being in my presence, one by one they were called into the portal—the hidden place they disappear—in my multidimensional world. At first, I believed I was just clumsy, lazy, or unaware, and that I had misplaced them. So, I decided to buy more rare and expensive specimens, thinking that would bring more attachment, care, and awareness on my part.

I was a make-up artist in Hollywood for a short period of time and had gone to a job at Fabio's Hollywood home. (Fabio was a well-known romance novel cover model turned mega icon in the 80s.) I had just bought a beautiful wedding-looking ring with a translucent, diamond cut, gem quality Moldavite, and was wearing it that day. The home was sparse but had a lovely little backyard with a patch of grass that looked out over the Hollywood Hills and was inspiring. I was there to do make-up for a woman who was interviewing Fabio for a news show, and I only briefly saw Fabio from across a room. At some point in the afternoon, the Moldavite ring slipped off my finger and into his lawn, disappearing into the portal as had all the others.

I was devastated and emotional, but I was sincerely trying to keep my cool as I searched the small backyard for my ring. Somehow, word got to Fabio, and he emerged from a side door of his home to help me look for it. The two of us walked in circles around each other on his little patch of grass. A splendid, thirty-six-year-old Fabio, his six-foot three-inch form, covered in a pair of his own brand of tight-fitting jeans with a white button-up shirt tucked in with a belt, billowing blonde hair falling to the center of his back— he was helping me look for my wedding-cut Moldavite ring. It was supremely unexpected and hilarious, so much so that I quickly began to let go of my sadness at the loss of the ring and money I had spent.

Neither Fabio nor I found the ring that night, but I felt firmly that it was at peace in the portal of his multidimensional Hollywood Hills home. Every piece of Moldavite I have ever had, I can still spiritually connect with—the asteroid-glass has a powerful connection to the Cosmos and all the extra-terrestrial relations that participate here on Earth. Moldavite was my first dedicated teacher to learning the art of detachment, and like all in the Andara family, no matter who you are and where you start, they will reawaken your spirit of mystery and surprise—along with fostering peace and kindness.

CRYSTAL GRID FOR EXPANSION

Working with a crystal grid is a simple way to begin connecting with the gem and mineral kingdom. You will need the following list of items for this specific grid. You can create a crystal grid by copying the one shown on the following page, on any material you would like: wood, metal, copper, paper, or cloth. Scan the QR Code on page 170 for the free grid download or go here: https://tracee-dunblazier.com/product/your-crystal-allies-the-12-best-gems-and-minerals-for-healing-trauma-and-navigating-change/.

Next, you will create a sacred altar space by cleaning and clearing an area in your home's main room or your bedroom, on which to place the grid. Write the intention for which you will build your grid and place it on the cleared altar space, under the grid. In addition to your grid, you can include a candle, a glass of water, and a form of offering of gratitude like tobacco, corn, or cornmeal. Now collect the stones listed below and place them on your grid.

This can be an active or passive ritual which means you can sit with your grid for a portion of time daily, weekly, or monthly (with consistency), or you may set up you grid and go about your life in a regular way. The grid words work with your subconscious and aligns you to the intention you have set forth. You will receive information in your meditation or mindfully on a daily basis.

You will need the following stones to create your Andara crystal grid.

- **Andara** for vision, placed in the center.
- **Opalite** for optimism and playfulness, placed above the center.
- **Lapis Lazuli** for firm and thoughtful communication, placed to the bottom right point.
- **Hematite** for grounding, placed on the bottom left point.

NOTES

NOTES

Scan the QR Code to Download Your Free Crystal Layout Grids

BIBLIOGRAPHY

Bradford, A. (2016). *Tantric Twin Quartz*. Retrieved from Crystal-Information.com: https://crystal-information.com/encyclopedia/tantric-twin-properties-and-meaning/

Cunningham, S. (1988, 1994). *Scott Cunningham's Encyclopedia of Crystal, Gem & Metal Magic*. St. Paul, MN, USA: Llewellyn Publications.

Donna Beaton. (2012). *Citrine from Zambia*. Retrieved 2022, from GIA: https://www.gia.edu/gems-gemology/citrine-from-zambia

Dunblazier, T. (2016). *Master Your Inner World: Embrace Your Power with Joy (The Demon Slayer's Handbook Series Book 1)*. Los Angeles: GoTracee Publishing, Inc.

Dunblazier, T. (2017). *Heal Your Soul History: Activate the True Power of Your Shadow (The Demon Slayer's Handbook Series Book 2)*. Los Angeles: GoTracee Publishing LLC.

Dunblazier, T. (2020). *Conquer Your Karmic Relationships: Heal Spiritual Trauma to Open Your Heart and Restore Your Soul (The Demon Slayer's Handbook Series Book 3)*. Los Angeles: GoTracee Publishing, Inc.

FireMountainGems.com. (n.d.). *Blue Lace Agate Meaning and Properties*. Retrieved 2022, from Fire Mountain Gems and Beads: https://www.firemountaingems.com/resources/encyclobeadia/gem-notes/gmstnprprtsbllc

Gross, W. R. (1905). *Kunzite the Precious*. Retrieved 2022, from Pala International: http://www.palagems.com/kunzite-the-precious

Hall, J. (2011). *101 Power Crystals: The Ultimate Guide to Magical Crystals, Gems, and Stones for Healing and Transformation*. Beverly, MA, USA: Fair WInds Press.

Hobart M. King, P. (2005-2022). *Citrine*. Retrieved 2022, from Geology.com: https://geology.com/gemstones/citrine/

Melody. (1995). *Love is In the Earth: A Kaleidoscope of Crystals*. Wheat Ridge, CO, USA: Earth-Love Publishing House.

Mineral Miners. (2020). *Phantom Quartz Crystal Information*. Retrieved from Mineral Miners: https://www.mineralminers.com/html/phqminfo.htm

NambianBlueLace.co.za. (2022). *Associations.* Retrieved from Nambian Blue Lace: http://namibianbluelace.co.za/inclusions/

Nanosital.com. (n.d.). *Nanosital.* Retrieved 2022, from Nanosital.com: https://nanosital.com/

Pearson, N. (2017). *Crystals for Karmic Healing: Transform Your Future by Releasing Your Past.* Rochester, VT, USA: Destiny Books.

Raphaell, K. (1987). *Crystal Healling: Applying the Therapeutic Properties of Crystals and Stones* (Vol. II). Santa Fe, New Mexico, USA: Aurora Press.

Raphaell, K. (1990). *The Crystalline Transmission: A Synthesis of Light* (Vol. III). Santa Fe, New Mexico, USA: Aurora Press.

Scialla, J. (2022). *A Brief History of Crystals and Healing.* Retrieved from Crystal Age: https://www.crystalage.com/crystal_information/crystal_history/

Simmons, R. (2009). *Stones of the New Consciousness: Healing, Awakening and Co-Creating with Crystals, Minerals and Gems.* Canada: North Atlantic Books, Heaven and Earth Publications.

Simmons, R., Ahsian, N., & Raven, H. (2005, 2007). *The Book of Stones: Who They Are and What They Teach* (Revised ed.). Canada: North Atlantic Books, Heaven and Earth Publishing.

Stonemania.com. (2022). *Blue Lace Agate from Ysterputz Southern Namibia.* Retrieved from Stone Mania: https://www.stonemania.co.uk/blog/blue-lace-agate-namibia

The Hollistic Science Company. (2022). *White Gold Essential Liquid.* Retrieved 2022, from The Hollistic Science Company: https://www.theholisticscienceco.com/white-gold-essential-liquid-ormus/

ABOUT THE AUTHOR

Tracee Dunblazier, GC-C, a Los Angeles-based empath, shaman, and 22-time award-winning author, has spent decades living an alchemical life working with crystal allies and using Transformative Grief as a guide. She was born multi-spirited, with a profound innate awareness of the spirit world and deep compassion for all who hurt. Tracee's down-to-Earth style embraces the humor of reality and has helped thousands to find radical acceptance, empowerment, and joy in their lives, no matter where they begin. Her national and international award-winning GoTracee Publishing creates spiritual tools that have become game-changers for those who suffer. Tracee is a charismatic keynote speaker and enjoys podcasting from her CHAT-Cast platform and currently serves as president of the Coalition of Visionary Resources, the trade organization for the Mind, Body, Spirit industry.

Other Books by Tracee Dunblazier